SIGNS AMID THE RUBBLE

SIGNS AMID THE RUBBLE

The Purposes of God in Human History

LESSLIE NEWBIGIN

Edited and Introduced by

GEOFFREY WAINWRIGHT

WILLIAM B. EERDMANS PUBLISHING COMPANY
GRAND RAPIDS, MICHIGAN / CAMBRIDGE, U.K.

© 2003 Wm. B. Eerdmans Publishing Co.
All rights reserved

Wm. B. Eerdmans Publishing Co.
255 Jefferson Ave. S.E., Grand Rapids, Michigan 49503 /
P.O. Box 163, Cambridge CB3 9PU U.K.

Printed in the United States of America

07 06 05 04 03   7 6 5 4 3 2 1

Library of Congress Cataloging-in-Publication Data

Newbigin, Lesslie.
Signs amid the rubble: the purposes of God in human history /
Lesslie Newbigin; edited and introduced by Geoffrey Wainwright.
p.   cm.
Includes bibliographical references.
ISBN 0-8028-0989-8 (pbk.: alk. paper)
1. Kingdom of God.   I. Wainwright, Geoffrey, 1939-   II. Title.

BT94.N46   2003
231.7′2 — dc21

2002192548

www.eerdmans.com

Contents

Editor's Introduction   vii

The Kingdom of God and the Idea of Progress

Bangalore Lecture I   3

Bangalore Lecture II   19

Bangalore Lecture III   31

Bangalore Lecture IV   46

The Henry Martyn Lectures

Authority, Dogma, and Dialogue   59

Conversion, Colonies, and Culture   78

Church, World, Kingdom   95

Gospel and Culture

The Gospel . . .   113

. . . and Culture   116

Editor's Introduction

GEOFFREY WAINWRIGHT

Lesslie Newbigin was a giant in the history of the ecumenical church of the twentieth century. By virtue of the range of his practical activities, the intellectual caliber of his writings, and the extent of his influence he most nearly invites comparison with the great fathers of early Christianity. Born in 1909 and raised an English Presbyterian, he served for over thirty years as a missionary in India, first as an evangelist, then as a bishop of the newly united Church of South India in the diocese of Madurai and Ramnad, and finally as bishop in the metropolitan area of Madras. Into the middle of his career he squeezed six years of service as general secretary of the International Missionary Council and then as director of the new division of world mission and evangelism at the time of the integration of the IMC with the World Council of Churches (1959-65). On retirement from India in 1974 Bishop Newbigin taught mission and ecumenism for five years at the Selly Oak Colleges in Birmingham, England. He then spent most of his eighth decade as pastor of a small congregation of the United Reformed Church in the racially and religiously mixed inner suburb of Winson Green across the city. Even when, towards the end of his days, he moved from Birmingham to South London, he busied himself until his death in 1998 with such varied interests as King's College in the University of London, the New English Orchestra, and the charismatic Anglican parish of Holy Trinity, Brompton. For the last twenty-five years of his long life, Newbigin's principal concern was the promotion of a "missionary encounter" with the modern Western culture that was spreading its tentacles across the globe, and he spearheaded the "Gospel and Our Culture" movement.

Lesslie Newbigin was a prolific author and lecturer in international demand. His published books number two dozen, and from his pen came a good hundred substantial articles in journals or chapters in composite works as well as many more casual pieces. In preparing my intellectual and spiritual biography of him, *Lesslie Newbigin: A Theological Life* (Oxford University Press, 2000), I nevertheless came across unpublished materials that for one reason or another seemed to me to merit publication, as given. Three sets compose this book.

The most important, biographically, is the series of four lectures that Newbigin delivered at the United Theological College in Bangalore in 1941 under the title "The Kingdom of God and the Idea of Progress." In his autobiography, *Unfinished Agenda,* he recalls that the lectureship gave him the opportunity to develop further some thinking on which he had already been engaged during his time as a graduate theological student at Westminster College, Cambridge. Lesslie himself pressed on me the significance of these Bangalore lectures as his first full treatment of themes that would continue to occupy him throughout his life. In them, Newbigin expounded the tension between the biblical story of mankind and the secular readings of history that had come to dominate the Western mind during the previous two or three centuries. In his archeology of the idea of progress, he stresses as a condition of its emergence the notion of linear time and the reality of worldly events as these are conveyed in the Bible; and then he shows how the idea had been not merely distorted but rendered incoherent or frankly false when, as happened in the rise of modernity, the transcendence of God as origin, sustenance, and goal of creation had been lost. In *Christian Freedom in the Modern World,* a book written on board ship during his first passage to India (1936), Newbigin — in the face of a picture of the world as "an upwelling blind process or urge," whether in "the Nazi philosophy of race and blood" or in "the Marxist materialist interpretation of history" — had allowed for a "profoundly different" idea of progress. On the Christian understanding, progress would be "based on the awareness that God can speak to us even in the sinful present, summoning us forward through the unconditional claims of duty to a better future"; this "better future" could include "the hopes and aspiration of the individual man," but Newbigin still located the prospect in the earthly history of humankind. In 1941, however, as "Christian" — or at least "progressive" — Europe found itself embroiled for the second time within a generation in a "world war,"

Newbigin insisted on a much more radical break between human capacity and achievement and "the kingdom of God."

Theologically, Newbigin's concerns in the Bangalore lectures fell under the heads of anthropology, soteriology, and eschatology. With the catechism of his church, Newbigin knew that "man's chief end is to glorify God and to enjoy him forever." He also knew that the will of fallen man was torn between good and evil, and that his very perceptions of the two were warped. Only in Christ had God graciously provided the revelation and redemption that could at least set human beings on the road to salvation. Between the historical road, both for each person and for the entire race, and the final divine goal stood the crisis of death and final judgment. In confrontation not only with the atemporality and individualism of Bultmann's current demythologization of the New Testament in an existentialist direction but also with the platonically inclined "eternism" of C. H. Dodd's "realized eschatology," Newbigin asserted both the fully real character of biblical eschatology, versus the reductively symbolic, and the constitutive value given by God to the present stage of salvation history as the prolepsis, but only the prolepsis, of the End. The new heavens and new earth that were to come as a final recreative act of God would provide the habitation of a transgenerational community of God's people — men and women raised in Christ from the dead — that avoided both the overprivileging of the later comers, as happened with any mundane idea of progress, and also the privatization of salvation which rescued particular souls in isolation from their human and historical context.

Newbigin's vision, then, in no way excluded or excused Christians from social and political engagement: Newbigin himself had read economics as part of his first degree at Cambridge, and under the tutelage of J. H. Oldham he had shared in the concerns of the ecumenical Life and Work movement around the theme of "church, community and state"; nor would he ever give up his own social and political interests and activities. But from the Bangalore lectures onward, he viewed the necessary Christian engagement in more "realistic" terms, as regards both its claims and its aims (he had heard Reinhold Niebuhr's Gifford Lectures at Edinburgh in 1939). Every action of the Christian, said Newbigin borrowing a dictum from Albert Schweitzer, should be a prayer for the coming of God's kingdom. Amid the dust and rubble of history — a phrase that has lost none of its power since Newbigin's use of it — deeds done for God's sake could, by God's transformative grace, one day show up perfected in God's final kingdom, for God "is able to keep what has been entrusted to him against that day" (2 Tim. 1:12). This is what gave grounds for hope as contrasted with the secular alternative to secular progress, namely a shorter- or longer-term nihilism. On that front also, Newbigin has a word to say to contemporary culture.

There is very little explicit ecclesiology in the Bangalore lectures. Newbigin's doctrine of the church would develop under the stimulus of his tasks as a negotiator in the final approach to the union of Anglicans, Methodists, and Reformed in the Church of South India (1947) and then as a bishop with "the care of all the churches." Springing from his defense of the South Indian pattern of unity in *The Reunion of the Church* (1948), Newbigin's treatise *The Household of God* (1953) quickly became an ecumenical classic. Both practical cooperation and spiritual fellowship fell short if not rooted in a visibly, organically united church, for division among Christians and their communities contradicted the very nature of the gospel, inflicted grievous bodily harm on Christ himself, and gravely impaired the church's mission in the world. While not seeing the World Council of Churches as the final form of Christian unity but only as an instrument of the churches on their way to reunion, Newbigin gave consistent support to the WCC in its heyday. He was a prominent figure at its first five assemblies and for two distinct periods a member of its commission on Faith and Order. He drafted the classic description, adopted at the New Delhi assembly in 1961, of "the unity we seek":

> We believe that the unity which is both God's will and his gift to his Church is being made visible as all in each place who are baptized into Jesus Christ and confess him as Lord and Saviour are brought by the Holy Spirit into one fully committed fellowship, holding the one apostolic faith, preaching the one Gospel, breaking the one bread, joining in common prayer, and having a corporate life reaching out in witness and service to all and who at the same time are united with the whole Christian fellowship in all places and all ages in such wise that ministry and members are accepted by all, and that all can act and speak together as occasion requires for the tasks to which God calls his people.

On his final return to Europe, Newbigin showed his disappointment at the slow progress towards unity among the home denominations. Not that his episcopal service in India had left him unfamiliar with the "local church" (far from it), but the local church now became also the center of his ecclesiological reflections (a fact not unconnected with his local pastorate in Birmingham's Winson Green). He had long held that "the church" as such was the "first fruits" or "foretaste," and therefore also the "sign" and "instrument," of the gospel and the kingdom, and he now emphasized the "hermeneutical" status and role of the local congregation in the desired missionary encounter with modernity. That would require hard intellectual work if the social, cultural, and religious challenges were to be met; and that is where Newbigin became heavily engaged in the study project of the British Council of Churches around the Orwellian year of 1984. His Henry Martyn Lectures — the second component in this book — are of a piece with his thinking that produced *Foolishness to the Greeks* (1986) and *The Gospel in a Pluralist Society* (1989), and they form part of the buildup to the Gospel and Our Culture movement.

Newbigin's Henry Martyn Lectures of 1986 belonged to a biennial series in honor of a brilliant young evangelical missionary who had gone out from Cambridge University to Asia in the early nineteenth century. Newbigin was returning to his own alma mater, where he had in his undergraduate years recovered his faith after youthful doubts, and from where, too, he had left for India in the mid 1930s. Settled back in England, retired twice over but by no means idle, he saw as the primary issue for mission the reconversion of the West.

The Henry Martyn Lectures show Newbigin setting about the liberation of contemporary Western Christianity from its complicity in the crisis of Enlightenment civilization, with its paradoxically self-asserting and self-undermining separation between public "facts" and private "values." There is no knowledge without a basis in some kind of belief, Newbigin argues, and every judgment is made within a particular worldview. The original gospel was preached as a proclamation of facts — of the incarnation of the divine Word as Jesus Christ, and of his ministry, death, and resurrection — which challenge every mundane value and set a final standard of truth. Without a recovery of nerve to preach that gospel, the church is failing in the mission with which it has been uniquely entrusted. With humility but no false modesty, the church listens, but it listens primarily to the Word, and only secondarily to the world in its self-assessed needs: already in a 1938 article on the "Under Thirty" page of the London weekly *The Spectator* the young Newbigin had declared that "the Gospel is something more serious than a solution to man's problems; it is a fresh and original word addressed to him from beyond the range of his problems by God, his maker."

In the wide-ranging Cambridge lectures Newbigin treats in their current form several topics on which he had long reflected: the nature of interreligious dialogue (from his first tour in India he had engaged with Hindu monks in the weekly study of the Upanishads and of the Christian Scriptures, and he was now becoming increasingly aware of the presence of Islam in Britain); the radical character of evangelical conversion, both personal and cultural, whereby any continuities between old and new can be perceived only in retrospect after the experience of disruption and redirection; the issue of language, not only in cross-cultural communication of the gospel but also where the gospel has lost its edge through domestication; the relation between verbal and practical testimony to the gospel (in a return visit to the CSI synod at this time Newbigin turned the epigram "Words without deeds are empty, but deeds without words are dumb").

At the end of the Henry Martyn Lectures, Newbigin returns to the question of the gospel and politics. In the 1960s, in line with his own belief in the public character of the gospel and the reality of human history under God, and following out some tendencies in his own Reformed tradition, Newbigin had briefly flirted with the "secular theology" of the day. By now, however, he has come back to the simultaneous propriety and sobriety of the Christian's engagement in politics. Dismissing inner-worldly utopianism, whether liberal-progressive or radical-revolutionary in kind, Newbigin writes a sentence that could have come directly from his Bangalore lectures of forty-five years earlier: "There is no straight line from the politics of this world, from the programs and projects in which we invest our energies, to the Kingdom of God." Yet there is room for "a movement of radical protest, suffering, and hope" — "under the sign of the cross and in the power of the resurrection" — in favor of "the new reality" that has broken in from above.

Not accidentally, the language of the Henry Martyn Lectures resonates strongly with the Fourth Gospel, on which Newbigin had published his long-matured commentary four years previously: "The Light

Has Come," and it shines on in a darkness that yet does not comprehend it; the Holy Spirit overturns the world's ideas of righteousness, sin, and judgment as these are displayed in its treatment of Jesus; and the crucified and risen Lord shows to His disciples His hands and His side and sends them into the world to preach the forgiveness of sins.

In December 1996 Newbigin was invited to the WCC's world conference on mission and evangelism at Salvador de Bahia in Brazil. His report on the meeting is printed in the April 1997 issue of the *International Bulletin of Missionary Research,* where with characteristic modesty he omits his own contribution. In fact, the Bishop was treated as an honored guest from yesteryear, but it seems that the organizers had not thought he would have much to say. His short address — now transcribed here — was fitted into two tight slots in a full program. At the close of the first session, when the moderator slipped him a note to say that his time was up, his failing eyesight prevented him — much to the delight of the assembly — from immediately getting the message. Before the second session, Newbigin had taken part in a dockside commemoration of the victims of slavery, and in the silence he had heard himself charged to raise the question whether the present generation of Christians, for their complicity in the practice of abortion, might one day be judged in the same terms as previous generations for their complicity in the slave trade. As a whole, the two-part address made a concise, eloquent, and passionate summation of Newbigin's convictions on a theme that had in one guise or another occupied him throughout his ministry: the relation between gospel and culture. It was his swan song on the ecumenical stage.

Until his eyesight failed, Newbigin's practice on formal occasions was to lecture from a rather complete text, and this, of course, is what has made possible the present publication of the Bangalore and the Henry Martyn Lectures. It is clear from the handwritten text of the Bangalore lectures in particular that Newbigin also at times either ad-libbed or inserted literary material, perhaps from other writings of his, perhaps by quoting from others. Newbigin's manuscript cues from Bangalore are here enclosed in square brackets. My own editorial conjectures about what came in those spots are offered in footnotes. They result from chasing up references to authors Newbigin mentions in the text and from consulting places in Newbigin's other writings where he treats the point in question.

For the release of all these texts thanks are due to the Newbigin family as literary executors, to William Neill-Hall as their agent, and to David Kettle as convenor of their advisory group. George Hunsberger, in whose custody the original manuscript of the Bangalore Lectures was kept, supplied a photocopy and a first attempt at transcription. I myself worked on the original manuscript of the Henry Martyn Lectures in the Selly Oak archives. Friends in Geneva located audio recordings of the address from Salvador de Bahia. Eerdmans were the American publishers of most of Newbigin's books during his lifetime, and Jon Pott has continued to favor the cause. Mary Ann Andrus struggled cheerfully with both Lesslie's handwriting and mine, as well as our English voices on tape, to produce an accurate basic text, and her enthusiasm for the substance and form of these materials is a testimony to Newbigin's continuing capacity to hold an audience. He, being dead, yet speaketh.

THE KINGDOM OF GOD
AND THE IDEA OF PROGRESS

Four Lectures by Lesslie Newbigin
Delivered at the United Theological College,
Bangalore, India

1941

Lecture I

If a visitor from Mars, that useful, if rather conventional, storehouse of impartial observers, could attend this course of lectures, I think the thing that would startle him most would be to find that a gathering of the sons of India, in the midst of that land which has been the home of so much of the world's profoundest religious thought, was discussing religious questions, not in their own language, but in the language of a tribe not noted for its piety, inhabiting a small group of islands on the northwest coast of Europe. If he went on to inquire into the origins of this surprising state of affairs, he would learn that during the brief period of three or four centuries the people of Europe, filled with a conviction that they were the born leaders of men, had spread themselves into almost every corner of the world, teaching their language, diffusing their ideas, selling their manufactures, building cities modeled on their own, and linking together into one unit of thought, trade, and culture peoples scattered throughout the whole world. He would find in Tokyo, Shanghai, Calcutta, Cape Town, Berlin, London, Chicago, and Buenos Aires cities with the same kind of buildings, the same kind of newspapers, and the same kind of ideas about what is important and what isn't. Looking a little closer, he would find that this was not the whole story. It would strike him that some strongholds of ancient ways of life had resolutely refused access to the new ways, the old plateau lands of Arabia and Tibet. Looking still closer in the ancient lands of Asia he would find that for every hundred who had given themselves wholly to the new way of life, there were a million who in their hearts utterly rejected it; that for every city like Madras, there were a thousand towns and villages where life went on essentially as before. But this would only bring out more clearly the distinctive character of this strange new city-civilization flung out over the whole world from the misty islands and coastal fringes of the European peninsula. If he went on to inquire what the prospects of this strange new civilization were, and journeyed to Europe, its focal center, to find out, he would have the biggest shock of all. We may picture him sitting in his concentration camp and listening to the roar of gunfire, the crash of explosions, the cries of tortured prisoners and the strident shouts of the mob orator and concluding that he had come, not to the center of civilization, but to the Dark Continent. He would feel like those Elizabethan explorers who set out to search for El Dorado, and found a cannibal island. And if he managed to escape and return to tell us his tale, I think the moral of it would be that we had better ask ourselves very earnestly whether this European civilization in which we are so much immersed has any future for it at all, whether we who almost unconsciously accept and follow the standards set by European civilization have not in fact got into the wrong bus.

I may say at once that I cordially agree with our friend from Mars in this general analysis of our situation's seriousness, and the course of enquiry which I propose for these four lectures will be an attempt to disentangle and criticize from a Christian point of view one of the seminal ideas of European civilization, the idea of progress. For we who are Christians are in this strange position that our Christian faith has come to us in large measure, though not entirely, in the dress of European civilization. This is simply a fact — it is not a matter of praising or blaming anybody. Christianity as a social phenomenon has always and necessarily been conditioned as to its outward form by other social facts. Christianity always comes to us first as somebody else's Christianity — our parents', our leaders', our friends'. For the great majority of Indian Christians it came as the Christianity of Europeans and inevitably took its shape from that. Now, when we see the terrible portents of our days, the almost complete obliteration of European civilization, for it is nothing less than that that we are witnessing, in the continent of its origin, it is a very pressing necessity that we should ask ourselves, in the light of the Christian revelation, wherein European civilization, that is to say our civilization, has gone astray. And I propose to direct attention to one of the focal ideas of European civilization — the idea of progress. The idea of progress is not the whole of European civilization, but it is a sort of lens through which the essential features of the whole can be seen.

Lecture I

Before we actually embark on the subject, some may wish to ask what bearing it has upon the ordinary business of Christian life and service. By the time we have finished, I hope the answer to that question will be clear; but by way of anticipation let me say just this. One of the constant tensions within the Christian fellowship for several decades has been the tension between the social gospel and the individual gospel, so called. Now what has been called the social gospel is, as I shall contend, the Christianized form of the idea of progress. In taking as our subject the Kingdom of God and the idea of progress, we are attempting to grasp, however falteringly, the fundamental theological issue which is at stake in this very familiar controversy. The idea of progress raises for Christianity in a very acute form the question of God's purpose for history as a whole. It is the difficulty of understanding the relation of this purpose for history as a whole, on the one hand, and God's purpose for the individual soul on the other, which makes the controversy between the individual gospel and the social gospel so difficult to solve. It is my hope that our study of this issue may help in some small manner to clear our minds on this very important and long-standing dispute.

In its very broadest terms, the idea of progress as we have become accustomed to it is the idea that human society has become better and will go on becoming better. It is the idea that ignorance and sin can be and will be gradually eliminated from human life, until a time shall come when men shall live together in perfect brotherly love, equipped with perfect knowledge. I know of no better expression of the idea of progress than the poem by John Addington Symonds which, strangely enough, is included in the hymnbooks of many Christian churches, including my own:

> These things shall be: a loftier race
> Than e'er the world hath known shall rise,
> With flame of freedom in their souls
> And light of knowledge in their eyes.
>
> They shall be gentle, brave, and strong
> To spill no drop of blood, but dare
> All that may plant man's lordship firm
> On earth, and fire, and sea, and air.

Nation with nation, land with land,
Inarmed shall live as comrades free;
In every heart and brain shall throb
The pulse of one fraternity.

Man shall love man, with heart as pure
And fervent as the young-eyed throng
Who chant their heavenly psalms before
God's face with undiscordant song.

New arts shall bloom of loftier mould,
And mighty music thrill the skies,
And every life shall be a song,
When all the earth is paradise.

Note that the idea of *man's* moral growth, and *man's* mastery over the world, are here central. Man is to become god-like; earth is to become paradise. And note also that this consummation is presented not as a hope only, or an aspiration, but as something which *shall* be — a destiny. These two points are fundamental to the whole idea of progress. Take first its estimate of man. Classical Christianity regarded man as a sinner, radically corrupt, unfit in himself for paradise. The idea of progress — in fact, modern European civilization — takes its stand on the belief that man is essentially good. The evil in man, it has generally said, is secondary — either due to environment, or simply to relative backwardness in the march of progress. In time it will disappear and man will shine forth in his true glory — gentle, brave, and strong. Hence in order to achieve progress, it is necessary to liberate man from the bondage of evil social institutions, and to educate him — that is, to draw out and train the essential goodness in him. And, secondly, it is a matter not merely of hope, but of certainty, that progress is a fact, and that it will lead in the end to the creation of a society of freedom, brotherhood, and peace.

This estimate of man, and this firm belief that history is an upward march, have been the sustaining and inspiring ideas of European civilization as we have known it. They set it apart decisively from the medieval society which went before it on the continent of Europe, and from the oriental cultures with which it competes in this and other lands. And now, at the moment of its greatest geographical expansion, it has collapsed in its own home base. Where and how did the idea of progress originate? According to J. B. Bury, it first appeared in France in the eighteenth century, but for the purpose of our study we may look further back and study the soil from which it sprang. The idea of progress can only exist where history is believed to be real. If you believe, as great masses of men have believed and do believe, that that which changes is unreal and that the real is the unchanging, then clearly you can have no doctrine of progress. The main intellectual tradition of the Greco-Roman civilization, and of Indian civilization, has been of this opinion. It has sought for the real in the changeless and has regarded the changeful world of history as relatively unreal. Consequently, it has regarded history not as a line of development leading to a goal, but as a wheel (*chakra,* in Sanskrit) ceaselessly arching round the center, which alone is at rest. This cyclical view of history — so widespread and influential in all ages — is of very great significance. I shall try to show that it is really an attempt to eliminate the distinctive thing in history, the historical in history, and to make it conform to the pattern of science.

Science deals with that which repeats itself and which can therefore be expressed in laws. Such laws are essentially timeless. Even if it be like the famous second law of thermodynamics, which teaches that the energy of the universe is being constantly spent, so that the universe is like a clock which is running down and cannot be wound up, even such a law transcends time in this sense that it is expressed as a law which is equally valid for all time, and which could leave no room for any future change in the process. In order to arrive at these laws, as is generally agreed, science abstracts from the actual world of things and happenings certain constant and recurrent features. On the basis of these it is able to formulate laws and so to make predictions about the future. But the fact that scientific prediction is incapable of solving for us one hundredth of the problems about the future which exercise us, proves that in abstracting that which suits its purpose, science has left behind a vast world of experience which it cannot express in terms of law. (I am aware that recent developments in atomic physics have raised questions as to whether law is fundamental to the work of science, but this does not invalidate the general account which I have given of the work of science as we have hitherto generally known it and as it has played and will continue to play its part in human thought.)

History, on the other hand, is precisely the account of remembered events in their full unrepeatable individuality. An event is important historically not when it illustrates certain general or timeless laws, but when, by its actual happening, it contributes in such and such a way to the development of a whole historical process. To describe events historically is to describe them as events which really happened and which have no significance at all if they did not happen. For science the question of whether this or that event really happened does not matter, provided the general law is not invalidated. Let me take an illustration from warfare. I have never read any textbooks of military science, but I suppose that they will contain numerous accounts of battles chosen to illustrate certain principles of tactics. The battles chosen will be those which illustrate these principles most clearly, and it would not matter if some battles were chosen from fiction, provided they clearly illustrated the truths to be taught. But in a strictly historical book the battles which are mentioned are those which actually altered the course of history, which by their issue determined a whole chain of subsequent events. Obviously in this case it makes all the difference in the world whether or not the battle really took place. If it be discovered that it did not take place, then the history books must all be rewritten.

Now the cyclical theory of history is really an attempt to do away with history in the sense above defined. It is the assertion that what seems to be individual and unrepeatable is really part of a cycle of repetitions — even though the length of the cycle is beyond human computation. It is an attempt to subsume the whole of history under a law or formula, and the fact that no evidence can be advanced in favor of the law only goes to show how strong are the forces in the human mind which urge men to formulate it. Once the changeless is accepted as the real, some such theory of history is the only possible one. No evidence is needed for it, because it is logically inevitable.

The biblical interpretation of history, on the other hand, is not circular but linear. It interprets history as a real process in which real events happen, events that is to say which have significance for God Himself. The biblical picture of God is not a changeless and impersonal absolute, but an active will, seeking, calling, leading, punishing, and forgiving. With this view of God there is no logical necessity for a circular view of history; on the contrary, history is accepted as real, the sphere in which the acts of God are accomplished and in which His will is being executed in judgment and mercy.

In India, where monistic thought is so dominant, I think the importance of this attitude to history is often not fully realized. It is often discussed, for instance, wherein the difference lies between the Christian and Hindu ideas of incarnation. But in the many discussions on this subject which I have listened to, I have never heard what seems to me the decisive difference pointed out — that the Christian dogma is a statement of historical fact which loses its entire importance if it is not an historically true statement, whereas the Hindu doctrine is a formulation of a supposed spiritual law analogous to the cyclical theory of history, and asking for no historical proof. The famous doctrine of the Gita that whenever virtue recedes and vice triumphs, Krishna becomes incarnate to re-establish virtue, is a statement on the model of the cyclical theory of history; and like it, it neither has any historical proof nor is felt to need any. The absence of any historical proof of the statement does not weaken its force for those who are within the Hindu worldview, because it is simply a deduction from that worldview. It does not matter whether this or that *avatar* is an historical personage or not. The fundamental religious idea is unaffected. On the other hand, if it be not historically true that in actual fact a person named Jesus lived, taught, died, and rose again in substantially the manner portrayed by the New Testament, then the whole claim of Christianity to be a revelation falls to the ground. In that case Christianity becomes, what the Vedantins believe that it is, just another version of the one and only religious truth. (In the third lecture I will discuss the sense in which history is real for God.)

This somewhat lengthy treatment of the difference between historical and scientific truth is necessitated by the rest of the argument. For it is clear that a worldview like those of India and of the ancient Greeks can have no place for and provide no opportunity for the idea of progress. Among the ancient peoples whose thought has come down to us, so far as I know, only the Hebrews and the Persians held a view of history from which the idea of progress could conceivably have emerged. For both of these, history was a real process, with a real goal. But that goal was "The Day of the Lord," not a natural consummation brought about by forces within human history, but a final victory of God over the powers of evil, and a final establishment of His Kingdom, His effective rule. Unlike the Greeks, therefore, the Hebrews and the Persians looked for their golden age to the future rather than to the past. But, at least as far as the Hebrew line of development is concerned, the hope that this golden age could dawn under the conditions of this world faded as the batterings of national and personal misfortune increased in intensity; it became more and more clear that God's Kingdom was something whose full realization lay beyond death and beyond this present age.

Medieval Christian Europe carried on the Hebrew belief in a Day of the Lord, and the Kingdom of Heaven, but the realization of these hopes lay very definitely beyond the river of death. That Kingdom was the object of all ardent hope and love, and to reach it was the goal of life. Life was a pilgrimage and men did not devote their energies to repairing the pilgrim road, but to reaching its end. There was no expectation, and no place for any expectation, that the world would become a better place. Not here, but there, in the heavenly country, was the haven of desire. For men who hoped, with a sure and vivid hope, that they would soon be treading the golden streets of Paradise, it was a matter of small moment that for a brief span of years they must pick their way along the muddy and refuse-sodden streets of a medieval town. The idea of earthly progress simply did not exist. [Insert][1]

1. No trace remains of the insert, but clearly it would have dealt with the rise of the idea of progress in the Renaissance, Early Modernity, and the Enlightenment. It seems likely that Newbigin would have drawn on the book he alluded to earlier by J. B. Bury, *The Idea of Progress: An Inquiry into Its Origin and Growth* (1932), which was dedicated to the memories of the Abbé de Saint-Pierre, Condorcet, Auguste Comte, Herbert Spencer, and "other optimists mentioned in this volume." Bury concluded his survey thus:

> Looking back on the course of the inquiry, we note how the history of the idea has been connected with the growth of modern science, with the growth of rationalism, and with the struggle for political and religious liberty. The precursors (Bodin and Bacon) lived at a time when the world was consciously emancipating itself from the authority of tradition and it was being discovered that liberty is a difficult theoretical problem. The idea took definite shape in France when the old scheme of the universe had been shattered by the victory of the new astronomy, and the prestige of Providence, *cuncta supercilio moventis*, was paling before the majesty of the immutable laws of nature. There began a slow but steady reinstatement of the kingdom of this world. The otherworldly dreams of theologians — "ceux qui reniaient la terre pour patrie" — which had ruled so long lost their power, and men's earthly home again insinuated itself into their affections, but with the new hope of its becoming a place fit for reasonable beings to live in. We have seen how the belief that our race is travelling towards earthly happiness was propagated by some eminent thinkers, as well as by some "not very fortunate persons who had a

Another line of thought powerfully reinforced the idea of progress. The rationalist Enlightenment of the eighteenth century culminated in a vision of apparently unlimited progress for the future. The Romantic Movement of the nineteenth century, taking the idea of *development* as its clue, searched the past for evidences that history is a record of the working out of laws of development. The idea was worked out in a myriad of different ways, but all had as their basic axiom the belief that history is a story of development from the crude to the refined, from the less to the more perfect. In contrast to the rationalism of the eighteenth century, which founded the hope of progress in the unlimited possibilities of the enlightened individual man, the romanticism of the nineteenth century concentrated its attention upon the group, nation, or tribe and professed to find within social history immanent laws of progress. The most daring and comprehensive of such philosophical constructions was that of the German philosopher G. W. F. Hegel, who taught that by a law of its own nature history moves forward from thesis to antithesis and synthesis after the model of the processes of human reasoning. His philosophy was used to buttress both the mystical nationalism of Russia and the dialectical materialism of Karl Marx, though it is probable that the structure of Marx's dialectic owes more to his Jewish religion than to his Hegelian philosophy.

But the most powerful stimulus which the idea of progress received in the popular mind of the nineteenth century came unquestionably from the Darwinian theory of evolution by natural selection. This biological account of the origin of species attained an enormous importance in the popular mind because it seemed to provide a scientific basis for the belief that progress — automatic and inevitable — was the law of life. That it does not do so we shall see shortly, but from the point of view of the history of the idea of progress, it is certainly true that for the average man Darwin's theory seemed to place the dogma of prog-

---

good deal of time on their hand." And all these high-priests and incense-bearers to whom the creed owes its success were rationalists, from the author of the *Histoire des oracles* [Fontenelle] to the philosopher of the Unknowable [Kant].

A more recent, longer-ranged, and theologically more astute account can be found in John Passmore, *The Perfectibility of Man* (1970).

Newbigin's own critical reading of the rise of modernity — with which the idea of progress is closely connected — underlies his *Foolishness to the Greeks: The Gospel and Western Culture* (1986), especially chapters 2, 4, and 5.

ress beyond the reach of reasonable doubt, so that those who doubted it could be dismissed decisively as obscurantist reactionaries.

Thus many distinct streams of thought contributed to the development of the idea of progress. Insofar as the idea still exists, it is more of the romantic than of the rationalist type. Only a few, like H. G. Wells, retain a belief in progress based upon the possibilities of the rational and enlightened individual. Much more widespread is the belief in various kinds of immanent laws of development by which history is supposed to be moving forward inevitably to this or that goal — the classless society, the New Order, or whatever it may be — and which are supposed themselves to provide their own criteria of right and wrong. Those who abandon themselves wholeheartedly to these movements — whether it be from positive enthusiasm for their professed aims, or from sheer despair of any alternative — seem to believe in them as movements of progress by which some good is to be realized. Those who cannot so identify themselves, because they retain certain standards of judgment which transcend the social process, tend to be more and more pessimistic and fatalistic as they see the world in the grip of these irresistible and non-moral forces of change.

Of course, like all popular ideas, the idea of progress has derived its power over the minds of men not mainly from the logical coherence of its argument, but from the fact that the ordinary conditions under which men lived and worked seemed to favor it. At least for those who were the beneficiaries of the capitalist system, the rapid increase of material wealth and the constant succession of new marvels in the world of applied science predisposed the mind towards an optimistic interpretation of history. If it had not been for this visible success, the idea of progress would never have become the self-evident idea which it did for masses of people. And in the same way, the disasters of the last twenty years have predisposed men to a pessimistic outlook and have therefore led to criticism of the idea of progress. Recognizing that this is the prevalent bias of our times, let us examine the arguments which have been used to support the idea of progress and see how far they are sound and how far fallacious.

We may take first the idea of progress in its most extreme form — the dogma that progress is a law of human history. Progress, as we defined it at the beginning, means a movement towards something better, something morally or aesthetically more desirable. Is there any proof that such progress is a law of history? We may grant that, provided society remains sufficiently stable, the growth of knowledge, and of man's mastery over nature, will be cumulative. But whether this growth will lead to progress as defined above, or to its opposite, depends upon other factors — the will of men to direct these greater powers to good or to evil ends. If man is essentially good, then growth in man's knowledge and in man's lordship of earth and sky and sea and air is progress. But if man is not good, but essentially sinful, this growth of power will lead him into deeper disaster. Thus unless this very large question is settled, the dogma of progress derives no clear support from the fact that knowledge is cumulative.

The attempt to find support for the dogma in the biological theory of evolution by natural selection is equally fruitless. [Insert]²

The same circular reasoning is involved in all attempts to establish the dogma of progress as an immanent law of the historical process. According to these theories there are immanent laws within human history which cause history to unfold through many stages towards perfection — just as there are laws immanent in the structure of a seed by which it develops into a great and noble tree. We can trace the working of these laws in the past, it is said, and we can be confident of their continued working in the future. In that case we must ask, from where do we derive the standard of good by which we judge that the historical

2. Again, no trace of the insert remains. Bury's *The Idea of Progress* devotes a chapter to "Progress in the Light of Evolution." Crucially: "In order to base Progress on Evolution two distinct arguments are required. If it could be shown that social life obeys the same general laws of evolution as nature, and also that the process involves an increase of happiness, then Progress would be as valid a hypothesis as the evolution of living forms." Bury cites Herbert Spencer's as "the ablest and most influential development of the argument from evolution to Progress"; but he himself notes that "upon the neutral fact of evolution a theory of pessimism may be built up as speciously as a theory of optimism" and cites on the other side E. von Hartmann, noting also that T. H. Huxley, "one of the most eminent interpreters of the doctrine of evolution," "did not, in his late years at least, entertain very sanguine views of mankind."

For Newbigin's views on modern biology, see again *Foolishness to the Greeks*, especially pp. 73-75, 91-92. At many points in his comments on the natural sciences, Newbigin contested the adequacy of efficient causality as an all-embracing "explanation" of things and advocated the recovery of the category of "purpose," which for him implied personal will. For the case made by two German thinkers, a philosopher and a scientist, see Robert Spaemann and Reinhard Löw, *Die Frage Wozu: Geschichte und Wiederentdeckung des teleologischen Denkens* (Munich: Piper, 1991).

process is a progressive one? For we are ourselves part of the historical process, so the development of our ideas of good and evil is itself a very important part of the historical process. If this standard of judgment comes to us from something or someone beyond the historical process, then the historical process is split in two — for man, who is part of the process, is in this very important matter independent of it. There is therefore no guarantee of any kind that the historical process is necessarily in the direction of greater good. But if, as more often happens, the proponents of this view refuse so to split the historical process, and claim that our developing moral judgments are themselves simply part of the working out of the immanent laws of history, then we make it impossible to claim that progress has taken place. If progress means movement from worse to better, and if our idea of what is better is itself derived from this movement, then to say that progress is a law of history is simply arguing in a circle. It amounts to this: We define what is good as what is in line with the development of society and then proceed to assert that the development of society is in the direction of the good. Obviously we have merely produced a tautology and proved nothing real at all. Yet this fallacy is plain both in Marxism and in all progress theories of an immanentist type. In fact, every argument for the dogma of progress as a law of history will be found to rest somewhere on a circular argument. At some point the vital question is begged; the thing which needs to be proved is quietly assumed. [Insert][3]

I pass to a second form of the idea of progress which does not claim that progress is a law automatic and inevitable, but states that progress has in fact taken place and may therefore reasonably be expected to go on taking place. If we look back over recorded history, through the dim mists of unrecorded prehistory, we cannot deny that very real progress has taken place. Consequently it is reasonable to hope that further progress will take place and to labor to that end. What shall we say of this more modest version of the idea of progress? We certainly cannot deny that there has been a vast increase in knowledge, in mastery over nature, in the development of refined and subtle techniques of thought and action. Consequent upon this there has been development in the size of human units, which in time opens up fresh possibilities. Again we can say that within certain periods there has been progress in the

---

3. No trace of the insert remains.

sense that certain evil customs and organizations were rooted out — dueling, slavery, human sacrifice, and so on. But we are learning today how very quickly victories so won may be lost again. The last ten years in Europe have seen the destruction of liberties won painfully over the course of a century. We have learned also that a victorious advance at one point in the battle line may expose the flanks to an unexpected and devastating counterattack and so lose more than it has won. David Livingstone's glorious dream, for which he suffered and toiled as few men have ever done, the dream of an Africa opened to missions and to a legitimate commerce which would eliminate the slave trade — that dream has been abundantly fulfilled. But with the fulfillment have come evils almost as bad as slavery — the utter disruption of African family life by the call of the mines, and the corrupting of the African with all the vices of the European. A hundred examples could be given to similar effect, and these drive us back to a re-examination of this idea of progress as a historical fact.

We defined progress as movement towards the good, the increasing realization of that which is in itself intrinsically good. But the only thing that can be called "good" in an absolute and unqualified sense is a good will. All other goods — good institutions, efficient instruments, sound organizations — may themselves become instruments of evil if those who use or conduct them do so for evil ends. The only thing which can be called good without this qualification is a good will, not an instrument, but a source of action steadily directed to good ends. Can we say that history is a progressive realization of the good in this fundamental sense? Is there any truth — is there any real meaning — in saying that Augustine was better than Socrates or Luther than Augustine? It is true beyond doubt that where stable social institutions have persisted for a sufficiently long time, we can in some cases discern progress in the sense that certain habits and social organizations are eliminated, and therefore removed from the range of choices among which the average man's will has to operate. But this is very far from being progress in the sense that we defined it above. Because slavery was part of the ordinary world of Paul's day and is not part of our ordinary world, Paul did not denounce it when he met it, whereas we do. But this certainly does not mean that we are morally superior to Paul. It means that by the labors of those who have gone before, certain evil possibilities have been largely removed from the range of immediate choice for the average human will. But, and here is the crux of the matter, the human will retains — in spite of all such developments — its paradoxical character as being capable at the same time of the most glorious heroism and of the basest evil. This is why it can and does often happen that what seemed like the assured gains of centuries may be thrown away in a few years of mad lawlessness. Which of us even ten years ago would have believed that in this year 1941, over large parts of Europe the profession of the evangelical Christian faith would require a man to carry his life in his hands every day? Who would have thought that in five years every single free institution in Germany, including even the family, could be practically crushed out of existence? Ten years ago men in Europe looked back to the Middle Ages as a time of darkness; now men look back to them as a time of light and reason compared to the black irrationality of our own age.

The true reading of history seems to be this, that every new increase of man's mastery over earth and sea and sky opens up possibilities not only of nobler good, but also of baser and more horrible evil, and that even those movements of social progress which can point to real achievement in the bettering of society have to be put side by side with these equally real movements of degeneration which have sometimes actually arisen out of the same social improvements. [Insert][4]

We have looked at the idea of progress firstly as the dogma that progress is the law of human development and second as the opinion that progress is a fact of past history. Let us conclude by looking at it in a third form, as a *faith* in the possibility of a better world in the future. This faith in the possibility of a better world has been the inspiration of much of the noblest heroisms of recent centuries. Its widespread breakdown has been accompanied by a distressing paralysis of moral effort in the sphere of politics and social life. No one should speak lightly of this belief in the midst of such tragic happenings. But what we have to ask is whether this faith has not broken down by the fact of its own falsity. For the moment we are considering the belief in its pure form, the belief namely that the aim of human life ought to be to work towards the coming of a perfect society on earth such as is pictured in John Addington Symonds's hymn. The Christian version of this belief we shall consider in our next lecture.

4. On some of the ambiguities of technological advance, see *Foolishness to the Greeks*, pp. 29-33.

The fundamental criticism of this belief, then, is that it violates what is generally felt to be the first commandment of ethics — that men are to be treated as ends and not as tools. However much of Kant's theory of religion we may reject, I think it is generally agreed that in thus formulating the fundamental law of ethics, he was right. Man is not to be treated solely as a means to an ulterior end — to an end, that is, which does not include his own fruition as a person. Now, if the hope of a future society which our contemporaries will never see is to be the whole spring and motive of their lives, the standard by which all they do is to be governed, then in asking them so to suffer and labor for it, we are making them means to an end which does not include their own personal fruition — in which they can have no part at all. This is not a matter of mere theory. [Insert: Koestler][5]

It is the peculiar tragedy of our times that those bright visions of earthly utopia which gladdened the eyes of men in the eighteenth and nineteenth centuries have led directly to the pitiless and dehumanizing idolatries of the twentieth. The enthusiasm for a better state of society on earth taken by itself has led us straight to the horrors of totalitarian Europe. With all its noble qualities it has failed even at its best to satisfy and integrate the whole human personality. And at its worst it loses all pity in zeal for an impersonal abstraction and makes of individual man only a blind social unit to be sacrificed in his millions upon the bloodstained altars of its idols.

There are other criticisms which may be made of the idea of progress; but what has been said has been sufficient, I hope, to show how extremely vulnerable has been this idea which has been so all important in the whole development of what we call European civilization. As regards the first two forms of the idea, the dogma of progress as a law of human society, and the opinion that progress is a fact of history, I hope that enough has been said to show that they were not sustainable. But the third form of the idea, the faith that progress is a possibility for the future, requires fuller treatment. Granted, it may be said, that a purely

---

5. Arthur Koestler's *Darkness at Noon* — a fact-based account of the "Moscow Trials" — was published in 1941. In later writings Newbigin would return again and again to the point that Marxism uses or discards successive generations in the process of creating a new world that they will never see. With especial clarity: "Stalinism is not an accidental outcome of Marxism, it is the logical development of it" (*The Open Secret*, 1978, p. 117; revised and expanded 1995, p. 104).

secular enthusiasm for earthly progress as the complete end of man is ultimately self-destructive and futile, may it not nevertheless be true that the Christian believing in God, believing in His rule over history, and believing also in a personal survival of death in which the full fruition of the individual is achieved, may work in this faith and in the promised power of the Spirit, to achieve a better state of society on earth? Is not this in fact a duty laid upon us by our Master?

What has been said already does not answer that question, and to it we must turn in our next lecture.

Lecture II

Christian belief about the future seems to be of two kinds, both of which may be present in one believer's mind, but which are nevertheless quite distinct. One is the belief that this world is going to be gradually subdued by the Spirit of Christ, working through His servants, until at last God's rule is complete and perfect, His will is done in earth as it is in heaven. This belief is often expressed in terms of the phrase "the Kingdom of God," and the prayer "thy Kingdom come" is understood as a prayer that this gradual process may be hastened. Questions concerning the general social progress of man, but somewhat distinct from questions of personal religion, are sometimes spoken of as questions of the Kingdom. I do not propose either to adopt or to criticize this usage at this stage, reserving what I have to say about Christ's teaching on the Kingdom to a later stage. It is sufficient that we should identify clearly this very widespread belief that the destiny of the world is that it should gradually be subdued and sanctified by the redeeming power of Christ so that at last a perfect state of society wholly obedient to God's will shall come to be on earth, and that the task of the Christian is to take his share in the accomplishing of this task. For convenience I shall refer to this as belief in progress.

On the other hand there is the view that the true object of hope for a Christian is a state of being beyond death, in which he will share with the whole communion of saints in the eternal bliss of the vision of God. To judge by ordinary habits of speech, the general thought seems to be that when each of us dies, he goes off, as it were, immediately and automatically to heaven, there to share in the perfect joy of God's presence. According to this view, earth and earthly life are essentially a place of training and testing by which the individual is prepared for the higher life beyond. Hope is not centered at all on this vale of tears where we spend our little span of years, but upon our true home in heaven to which we go when our time of conflict and testing is successfully passed.

I have stated these two views boldly and perhaps unsympathetically simply because I want to define them clearly for our minds. In fact, as we all know, these two ideas are generally present in varying proportions in the minds of all Christians. No one, if questioned, will say that a Christian's only interest is in heaven and that the bettering of this world is of no interest to him whatever; on the other hand, no Christian will deny that man has some destiny beyond death, and that therefore his whole significance is not exhausted by his share in the realization of a process of social progress. We acknowledge intellectually, that is to say, that neither of these beliefs is satisfying by itself; yet we cannot effectively combine them. Stated clearly and boldly, they are mutually contradictory. It cannot be true at one and the same time that the significance of human history as a whole is that it leads to the Kingdom of God on earth, and that the significance of human life individually is that it leads to fullness of personal fruition in the Kingdom of Heaven beyond death. The two cannot be held simultaneously as real articles of living, active faith. It is this, I believe, which creates the real controversy between what we loosely call the social gospel and the individual gospel. A man may try for argumentative purposes to combine elements of the two beliefs into some sort of coherent statement, but when it comes to the question where the real center of his hopes and strivings lies, it must be in one or the other: it cannot be in both at once. Either the hope of heaven will be a faint and shadowy thing, at least in the years when we regard death as too far away to be a matter of real concern, and we shall pin our ardent hopes to the bettering of human society. Or we shall pay mere lip service to the idea of earthly progress, and devote our energies to the task of preparing ourselves and others for our real destiny in a better world beyond death. If it really be true that the two beliefs we are discussing are the only possibilities open to us, then we seem shut up to an insoluble dilemma.

Consider more closely these two alternatives and see how untenable each by itself is, and how impossible it is to combine them together. Take first the belief in Christian progress. We have seen in the previous lecture how vulnerable to criticism the whole idea of progress is, and indeed how untenable it is whether as a dogma, an opinion, or a faith. And there can be no doubt, historically speaking, that the popular Christian doctrine of the Kingdom of God, interpreted as meaning the progressive realization of good in the life of the world, is simply a Christianized version of the secular idea of progress. It is, I think, the general conclusion of a very wide range of modern students of the Gospels that on Jesus' lips the phrase the Kingdom of God did *not* refer to a gradually developing historical progress culminating in the establishment of a perfect society on earth. But quite apart from this, it would be a very remarkable thing if the real meaning of the very central phrase of Jesus' teaching should have remained entirely hidden for seventeen centuries until it was discovered by a group of French rationalist philosophers who were not interested in the New Testament at all. We must, I think, candidly admit that the idea of earthly progress towards a Kingdom of God on earth cannot possibly be derived from the Gospels by themselves, but is the interpretation of the gospel teaching by men who came to it with minds molded as to their whole preconceptions by the secular idea of progress. I think that is simply an historically true statement.

But, it may legitimately be argued, the fact that this idea of Christian progress has such and such origins does not prove it untrue. It may be that whereas the secular form of belief in progress is false, the Christian form of the belief is true. Certainly the criticisms made yesterday of the idea of progress as a dogma of history would not be valid against a form of the dogma which derived it directly from the revealed character of God in Christ. But it is more than doubtful whether such a dogma can really be derived from the New Testament revelation, which is so very far from being optimistic about future earthly developments. The criticisms made of the opinion that progress is a fact of history are as valid against the Christian idea of progress as against the secular. The Christian holds that every man, whatever the level of his ethical achievements, stands in need of a fundamental conversion. In this matter every man and every generation stands on the same level, and not on the shoulders of the generation before. The Pharisees, the climax of a wonderful process of moral and spiritual development by which a whole nation had been raised to hitherto unknown levels of spirituality and ethical purity, were themselves — according to Christ — more desperately in need of that conversion than any others. The Christian has no more grounds than any other for asserting that progress is a fact of history.

But what about the third form of the idea of progress, the faith in progress as a future possibility? Even if the secular reformer has no valid ground for this faith, may not the Christian find valid grounds for it in the Christian revelation of God's nature and will? Once more I am not at this stage discussing New Testament evidence: it will be sufficient to point out two fatal objections to the idea that the proper goal of Christian effort is the perfect society, the Kingdom of God on earth. I am in this assuming the Christian belief in personal immortality or resurrection.

Firstly, it means that there are in our scheme of things two perfect societies. One is a perfect society on earth from which all but the final generations are shut out, and where they enjoy the perfection which they have not striven for but simply walked into; the other is a perfect society beyond death, where all the preceding generations who are balked of that earthly kingdom which they strove for enjoy, as a kind of reward for their labors and as a substitute for their disappointed hopes, the bliss of heaven. Now this has only to be stated in order to be condemned as nonsense. Yet I do not see how else we can state with precision the implication of the common Christian belief in a Kingdom of God on earth as the goal of progress. There are in the Christian faith certain paradoxes which cannot be resolved intellectually but must be held onto because the mind intuitively realizes that the paradox as a whole is nearer the truth than any purely rational statement could be. But this is not such a paradox. It is a sheer self-contradiction which we cannot rest in for a moment when we clearly understand it. If to seek the Kingdom of God means, as is often said, simply to labor for the coming of a perfect society on earth and not to bother about heaven, and if heaven be the place where those who have faithfully striven on earth go to when they die, then the Christian's fate is to seek that which he is absolutely debarred from ever finding and to find that which he is advised not to seek. Which, as the geometry books say, is absurd.

Secondly, we have to question the very idea of a perfect human society under the biological and spiritual conditions of human life as we know them. As long as man is a biological organism subject to the usual law of decay and death, then perfection as our spirits thirst for it is unattainable. I am not thinking simply of the fact of death itself, with all

22

the pain and sorrow associated with it — though that is a very large inroad upon the idea of perfection. I am thinking of that fact of human life of which death is the final symbol, that transience and impermanence by which every present joy turns even as we enjoy it into a dead and irrecoverable past. This fact of transiency, this poignant sense of constant and irrecoverable loss which comes upon us when we are brought to realize that we shall never see some friend again, and never visit some well-loved place again, never share again in some experience of work or enjoyment which has been very precious to us: this factor of transiency, I say, is part of the very stuff of life, but we know that our spirits chafe against it, and that they only overcome it insofar as they are lifted up in lively faith and hope of a world where these things are so no more. A society existing under these biological conditions of decay and death is not a perfect society and cannot satisfy the spirit's thirst for perfection.

Not only so, but the idea of a perfect society on earth conflicts with another fact of human nature as we know it. Human nature, in every form that it has been known, requires struggle and effort in order to achieve character. Mere happiness unrelated to such struggle, unearned comfort and ease, corrupts and does not enable. We are such that we need to strive for that which we enjoy. A world from which all evil has been banished, leaving no problems for men to struggle with, and offering simply a lifetime of cultured ease such as most visions of earthly perfection suggest to us, would be a world where humanity as we know it would decay. That is why all pictures of the perfect earthly society are so banal and unsatisfying. All attempts, in fact, to picture a perfect human society under earthly conditions suffer shipwreck on the facts of man's biological and spiritual nature.

For these two reasons, then, we conclude that we cannot accept as it stands the belief that the aim of a Christian life is to work towards the creation of a perfect society on earth.

We turn, therefore, to the other apparent alternative, the belief that the aim of a Christian life is to be found in another world which one enters by the act of dying. This very prevalent type of belief is open to criticisms along at least three lines.

Firstly, it is untrue to the whole Christian idea of salvation. It centers attention upon individual redemption out of the world rather than upon the redemption of the world. We are very familiar with the many *marga*s or paths which Hinduism offers to the seeker after salvation. Each one offers a way by which the individual may pull himself from the bonds of worldly existence and enter — as an individual — into the experience of release. But the gospel as proclaimed in the New Testament is something very different from this. It is the publication of the divine plan to sum up all things in Christ — according to St. Paul's definition. The hope set before us in the gospel is fundamentally corporate, not individualistic. To imagine that the individual soul may, so to speak, simply quit the whole travail and labor of God's purpose in the world and enjoy a merely individual experience of heaven seems to be untrue to the spirit of the gospel. We can certainly believe that there is for the individual a higher and more blessed sphere of service beyond death, but I do not think we can believe that the individual can enter into the full blessedness of God's Kingdom apart from the full consummation of that Kingdom as it concerns all men, and all creation. It is of the essence of that Kingdom that its joy is the joy of communion. That joy cannot be complete till the fellowship is complete. It awaits, therefore, the full completion of God's purpose. We know that it is one by one that men must yield their obedience to God. But the full end of the obedience, the entry into the joy of God's perfected family, must necessarily be the act and experience of all together, and not one by one. The Kingdom cannot be enjoyed in full till all share it, because it is the Kingdom of love.

Secondly, this purely individualistic conception of the Kingdom robs human history as a whole of its meaning. According to this view, the significance of life in this world is exhaustively defined as the training of individual souls for heaven. Thus there can be no connected purpose running through history as a whole, but only a series of disconnected purposes for each individual life. History, on this view, would have no goal, no *telos:* it could only have, so to speak, a full stop when the last individual soul had left it for the heavenly world and its business as a training ground for souls was done. If he completely accepted this view, a man could not throw himself wholeheartedly into some forward-looking program of social betterment, because his worldview would allow no significant place for social betterment. His one concern would be the preparing of himself and others for their destiny in heaven. The existence of world history as a whole would remain an inexplicable mystery.

Thirdly, this view in practice leaves man without any guidance in the vast majority of the actual problems of life. It is the distinctive character of our modern world that the technical conditions of production and distribution have knit men together as far as most of their activities are concerned into larger and larger units. In the pre-mechanical age the vast majority of the practical dealings of life were direct and personal. The relations of employer and employee, buyer and seller, teacher and student, writer and reader, were, in the main, relations between people who knew each other as persons. The problems of life presented themselves almost entirely as problems of personal relations within a relatively stable social structure. For the right ordering of these relations the one essential was a right view of man's personal nature and destiny. So long, therefore, as these conditions prevailed, the type of eschatology which concentrates almost exclusively upon the destiny of the individual could provide the guidance needed for most of the practical issues of life. There was a fairly clearly understood system of principles for the guidance of the Christian in the affairs of his daily life.

But we in the twentieth century are living in a profoundly changed world. The food we eat, the clothes we wear, the books and newspapers we read and the opinions they propound are the products of vast industrial and financial groupings which control resources often greater than those of a medium-sized state. Consequently in the vast majority of our actions, buying, selling, earning our living, reading and listening, we are dealing not with individuals whom we know personally but with vast anonymous organizations, controlled ultimately by people whom we have probably never heard of, and who may be living thousands of miles away. And insofar as this is so, a system of conduct based simply on individual character and individual destiny is powerless to control life as we actually know it. Life as we know it can only be controlled — if it can be controlled at all — by political means and in terms of a political and social purpose. Take, for instance, the basic problem of ordinary life — employment and unemployment. The ordinary principles of personal character and conduct are practically irrelevant to this problem. The vast mass of unemployment is not due to the personal defects of the unemployed or of the employees and cannot be remedied by remedying these defects. It is due to forces over which they have — as individuals — no more control than they have over the phases of the moon. It can only be controlled by political power exercised on the basis of a definite view of the purpose of society as a whole. A worldview which simply concerns the destiny of the individual and has nothing to say about the destiny of society as a whole has, strictly speaking, no guidance whatever to offer on a problem like unemployment. That is why only the totalitarian states, which have a definite theory of society, have been able to control employment and unemployment. Without some such theory of society as a whole, the problem is as far removed from human control as the operations of a volcano.

I have taken unemployment as one example, but it is of course only one among hundreds which might be taken. Indeed the central problem of our age is just this, that the technical conditions of production, trade, and finance require enormous units of organization and that such units can only be controlled in the interests of society as a whole by enormously strong and unified political power. This centralization of political power in turn is only possible on the basis of some commonly acceptable view of the social purpose, for the sake of which people will surrender their liberties to this central control. So far the totalitarian countries have achieved this control but on the basis of a social theory which destroys all freedom. The problem is to find a basis and method of centralized control which shall not destroy freedom. If Christians have nothing to say about the destiny of society as a whole, then they have nothing to say about the central problem of our civilization and about three-fourths of the workaday life of the ordinary man.

For these three reasons, then, we cannot rest content with the purely individualist view of man's destiny. Somehow or other we have to find a view which does justice to both aspects of the problem — individual and social — and which resolves the apparent contradictions between them. Enough has, I hope, been said to make it clear that whatever the solution may be, it cannot be very simple. When we face fully the difficulties involved in both the individualistic and the social types of eschatology, we understand, I think, why the eschatological teachings of the Bible are sometimes so extraordinarily complicated. We are dealing with a problem for which there are no simple solutions.

We turn, then, to the New Testament teaching on the problem of eschatology. And let me confess at once that I am not proposing to make any detailed study of this because I am not competent to do so, and because the subject has engaged the attention of students of the New Testament so much in recent years that it is not to be expected that an amateur in this field can add anything new. I wish merely to remind you of the main conclusions which have emerged from recent study of the New Testament and especially of the Gospels.

The background of the New Testament teaching is the conception of the Kingdom of God as both the fact of God's rule and the sphere of His rule. It is both His kingly authority, and His royal domain. As the sphere of His present rule it is the transcendent Kingdom of Heaven where already ministering spirits obey perfectly His perfect will. As His kingly rule on earth it is future — eschatological. That is to say, the Kingdom of Heaven is to *come* on earth in the sense that this existing age is to be terminated and the divine sovereignty which is now effective in heaven is to become effective on earth. The whole present order, characterized by the triumph of evil forces, by corruption and death, is to be replaced by the heavenly order, characterized by the sovereignty of God and the abolition of corruption and death. In the new age the old orders will be gone, even the order of marriage. Men will be as the angels in heaven now are.

Note that this is essentially a corporate hope. The Kingdom is not a place where men go to one by one when they die. The Jewish name for that place was Sheol — the place of shades where men praise not Jehovah. No, it was the expectation of a new age, a new world under a new heaven and a new earth. It is not universalist, for the prelude to it is the destruction of the organized forces of wickedness, but neither is it individualist. It is social and cosmic, concerning men as a whole, and not only men but the whole created world also.

Such is the Hebrew background: and the central proclamation of the New Testament is that in Christ the new age has already dawned. In the words of the very first proclamation of the gospel, "The Kingdom of God has come near." In Christ the powers of the new age are at work. The domain of Heaven has touched that of earth and God's rule is actually being exercised in the world through Jesus. Those who accept Him come within the sphere of operations of the powers of the Kingdom: they may in fact be said to have been translated out of the present age into the new age which is to come. The new age is no longer something in the distant future. It is already present proleptically. Christians have already, as it is said, tasted the powers of the age to come.

Or, using the metaphor of space instead of that of time — they are said to be a colony of heaven, an outpost of the transcendent Kingdom of Heaven within the ordinary world of men. This is the state of belief which C. H. Dodd calls "realized eschatology" — the state, that is, in which those last things which are the subject matter of eschatology are believed already to have come to pass. They are no longer matters of a distant future: they are realized facts. "On us," as they said, "the end of the ages is come." But of course at the same time along with this realized eschatology there was a futurist eschatology as well. The phrase "realized eschatology" can only be used properly if the word 'eschatology' is, so to speak, put in inverted commas. For obviously, in the strict sense, the last things have not yet come to pass: the world still goes on. Consequently, men are bound still to speculate on the end to which history is moving. Such speculation is eschatology properly so called — that is, futurist eschatology. This point is worth making because Dodd seems to deplore futurist eschatology as a declension from the genuine eschatology of the Gospels and of Jesus, which was realized eschatology. Some kind of futurist eschatology there had to be and must always be. Its character was necessarily governed by what they had already tasted of the powers of the age to come, but it is unquestionable that the first Christians did look forward as well as back.

What, then, was the character of this futurist eschatology? It was the expectation that the coming of Jesus into the world, by which the character of God's Kingdom had been once for all revealed and its powers set free among men, would be speedily completed by His second coming to judge the world and finally to establish and complete God's Kingdom. Three main features of this New Testament eschatology may be noted.

Firstly, it carries on the Old Testament belief in a cosmic renewal or restoration. It is neither to an otherworldly heaven, nor to a gradual improvement of earth that the New Testament looks forward, but to a divine act by which all created things are to be renewed. The Kingdom of God is to come down out of heaven so that God's will is done in the whole domain of earth as it is now done in heaven. It is to be a new Jerusalem, a human commonwealth with all its appurtenances newly created according to the divine will. In all this the New Testament carries forward these prophetic and apocalyptic hopes of the Hebrews which began with the ardent but humble hope of the restoration of the kingdom of David and led up to the growing hopes of a restoration of God's rightful sovereignty over the whole world. But in two ways the New Testament modified these Old Testament hopes. In the first place, the character of God's rule had been clearly revealed. It was the rule of the God and Father of our Lord Jesus Christ that settled the character of legitimate expectations about the coming Kingdom. In the second place, the powers of the new Kingdom were already at work. Jesus by His life and death and resurrection had broken the hold of evil upon those who accepted Him. Those who were "in Christ" were already citizens of the New Jerusalem, even though still living in the old world. Thus the Kingdom, though future, was not merely future; its characteristic life of freedom in the service of God was already in a real sense a present experience also.

The second main point to be noted about the New Testament eschatology is that the full establishment of the Kingdom is first of all a day of judgment. The return of Christ is a return as judge. This idea of a day of judgment at which men will be judged according to their deeds and by which their ultimate admission to or exclusion from the blessed Kingdom will be decided, is quite vital to the New Testament eschatology. It is found both in the teaching of Jesus Himself and in the Epistles. It is especially noteworthy that in that epistle of Paul — Romans — which is chiefly concerned to establish the doctrine of justification by faith, not by works, the belief in a final judgment on men according to their works is also quite clearly brought out.

In the third place, according to the New Testament eschatology the relation between our present life in this world and our life in the new world of the Kingdom is understood in terms of death and resurrection. The resurrection of Christ from the dead is itself the proof of God's purpose for those who believe in Christ. Christ is called the first fruits of them that sleep, and it is added that as Christ was raised so shall they that are Christ's be raised at His coming. It is true that in other contexts it is said that Christians have already died and been raised with Christ, so that their life in this world is a kind of resurrection life. But this is precisely an example of the way in which the New Testament sees the Kingdom both as future and also as proleptically present in the experience of believers of the Kingdom of God. The actual literal fact of resurrection is a future hope for believers, just as death as a literal experience is also future. But in the death and resurrection of Jesus they have a solid accomplished fact which makes this hope not faint but certain and so enables them to taste now — by faith — the life of the Kingdom which awaits them.

And the point is that that life is not just an extension of this life in the corruptible body of humanity. This life is under sentence of death. No conceivable extension of it could fit it for participation in the new kingdom. It is doomed to die — to see corruption complete its work. The physical frame, the personality as we understand the term, all achievements in personal character and in social effort — all is doomed to be lost in the dust of history. But yet, by a miracle of which the sprouting of corn from the buried seed is a faint analogy, a new life is given by God — a resurrected life fit for the new age.

The Second Coming, the New Age, resurrection, judgment — these are the cardinal ideas of the New Testament eschatology. How far do they answer for us the problem which prompted these studies?

Lecture III

I have said that the eschatology of the New Testament centers on the ideas of the Second Coming of Christ, the end of the world, as we know it, and the ushering in of the Kingdom of God by resurrection and judgment. No one who is expounding the New Testament can quite get away from these ideas. But I think it would be true to say that they are not the ideas which occupy the center of the consciousness of the average Christian of our day as he looks forward; and as I have already said, it is the two ideas of personal immortality and gradual social progress which tend to jostle one another in the forefront of men's minds when they think about things. It is moreover a striking fact that those New Testament scholars who have very clearly redirected attention to the eschatological character of the Kingdom as it is portrayed in the New Testament nevertheless shrink very noticeably from taking literally the ideas of a catastrophic end of the world — resurrection and judgment. Rather are those ideas treated as being symbols of certain abiding facts of the spiritual life. The idea that on some particular day — it might be tomorrow — at a particular time, world history is going to be brought to an abrupt end, seems to many people intolerable. Things like that do not happen!

Sayings in the New Testament which speak of such an end of history are not, these scholars say, literal statements of future events: they are symbolic statements of spiritual truths, the truth — for instance — that all history and all events are equally under the judgment of God. Similarly the idea of a Day of Judgment when the righteous will be publicly vindicated and enter into their reward while the evil will be — as it is said in the Gospels — sent away into everlasting punishment, is felt

31

by very many to be intolerable if taken literally. To imagine such a literal judgment may, they say, imply that God finally loses patience with the slow travail of human history and decides, so to speak, to terminate the process by writing off part of the human race as a total loss and accepting only partial success in His purpose. Rather than believing in a literal Day of Judgment, therefore, we ought to understand the picture of the judgment day as symbolic of the eternal spiritual fact that we all stand perpetually under the judgment of God.

Let us consider three objections to the idea of a literal last day.

I

It is interesting to note that C. H. Dodd, who has done so much to direct attention to the eschatological nature of the Kingdom of God in the gospel preaching, yet at the same time very clearly shows that he regards the eschaton as a symbol and not as a literal fact. (This is a thing we often see in theology, and it is often very perplexing. A scholar will on the one hand emphatically underline a certain aspect of the gospel story, and on the other hand proceed to qualify all that he has said by explaining that he understands it symbolically and not literally. What he does with one hand as an exegete, he undoes with the other as a theologian.) [Digression: Miracles][1]

Dodd brings out with the utmost clarity the fact that eschatology is fundamental to biblical thought and for the thought of Jesus. But in interpreting eschatology exhaustively as realized eschatology, he makes it formal and symbolic rather than factual. In Jesus, he says, the eschaton

---

1. What Newbigin is likely to have said about miracle can be surmised from what he characteristically said on many future occasions about the resurrection of Jesus. For example: "That the tomb was empty . . . can be accepted as a fact only if the whole plausibility structure of contemporary Western culture is called into question. To accept it as a fact means that history has a meaning that cannot be found from any study of the regularities and recurrences of the past. It means that the whole existing order of nature and history is confronted by a new reality that gives it a new meaning" (*Foolishness to the Greeks*, 1986, p. 62). Or, with a sideswipe at Rudolf Bultmann's notorious essay of 1941 on "The New Testament and Mythology": "It is no more and no less difficult to believe in the resurrection after the invention of electric light than before. . . . It has never been possible to fit the resurrection of Jesus into any worldview except a worldview of which it is the basis" (*Honest Religion for Secular Man*, 1966, p. 53; cf. *Truth to Tell*, 1991, p. 11).

entered into actual human history. And the eschaton is always present as judgment, death, and resurrection for each moment of history. It is a new, vertical dimension by which history is constantly being judged and re-created. Thus the Christian's duty is not to rest hope on the unrealized future: the future can give us nothing that we have not already got. Our duty is to seek perfection now at every moment in concrete obedience to the will of God. By so doing one is living in the eschatological order. [Quotes][2]

In all this it is quite clear that the eschaton has ceased to be, literally, the end of history — that is to say, an unrealized future event — and has become exclusively a symbol for certain spiritual experiences of the Christian life. Now it is of course plain that the only significance of eschatology, as of any other doctrine, is its bearing upon actual life and thought now. The eschaton, the end, enters into our present experience

2. The work of Dodd's that Newbigin criticizes for its lopsided emphasis on realized eschatology will be his *Parables of the Kingdom* (1935). Here Newbigin seems particularly to aim at chapter 3 ("The Day of the Son of Man"). The likely passages for quotation are these:

> Jesus declares that . . . the Kingdom of God has come into history, and He takes upon Himself the "eschatological" role of "Son of Man." The absolute, the "wholly other," has entered into time and space. And as the Kingdom of God has come and the Son of Man has come, so also judgment and blessedness have come into human experience. . . . The historical order, however, cannot contain the whole meaning of the absolute. The imagery therefore retains its significance as symbolizing the eternal realities, which though they enter history are not exhausted in it. The Son of Man has come, but also He will come; the sin of men is judged, but also it will be judged.
>
> But these future tenses are only an accommodation of language. There is no coming of the Son of Man "after" His coming in Galilee and Jerusalem, whether soon or late, for there is no before and after in the eternal order. The Kingdom of God in its full reality is not something which will happen after other things have happened. It is that to which men awake when this order of time and space no longer limits their vision, when they "sit at meat in the Kingdom of God" with all the blessed dead, and drink with Christ the "new wine" of eternal felicity. "The Day of the Son of Man" stands for the timeless fact. So far as history can contain it, it is embodied in the historic crisis which the coming of Jesus brought about. But the spirit of man, though dwelling in history, belongs to the eternal order, and the full meaning of the Day of the Son of Man, or of the Kingdom of God, he can experience only in that eternal order. That which cannot be experienced in history is symbolized by the picture of a coming event, and its timeless quality is expressed as pure simultaneity in time — "as the lightning flashes" (pp. 107-8).

by qualifying all present action; that is its significance. But the point is whether it does not lose that significance unless it be also a fact which is really going to happen. For example, the fact that we are all destined one day to die, has profound significance for every day of our lives: it qualifies them in all sorts of ways and gives to them their peculiar quality. But that does not mean that death can be treated exclusively as a formal and symbolic idea which is equally present to qualify all being. It derives its power to qualify all being from the fact that it is known to be a future certainty, as an actual fact which will really happen some day. Take away the literal fact, and the symbol vanishes. Mortality is a present fact because death is a future certainty in the same way, it seems to me, that all talk about eschatology as an element in Christian thinking is a mere beating of the air, unless it be really the case that some day there is really going to be an eschaton. Only if there be real belief that an end is coming, will that end qualify what goes before it with the peculiar beliefs and feelings which we call eschatological. The eschatological in Christian experience is the shadow of the eschaton cast backwards across time, but if the eschaton is itself non-existent, then the shadow must disappear.

Belief in eschatology without belief in a literal eschaton is like belief in religion without belief in God — because "religion stands for certain valuable principles and therefore should be preserved." [Expand][3]

We must ask why the idea of a real end of history is felt to be intolerable. Partly because it is something never experienced. Fundamentally, however, it is due to the belief that time cannot be a reality for God. This is a place where the Greek philosophical tradition has profoundly, and I believe disastrously, deflected Christian thought off biblical lines. For those deeply influenced by that tradition (and Hindu tradition), it is an axiom that all time — past, present, and future — is equally present to God. This, it is felt, is the only view which is congruent with belief in divine omniscience and perfection. If God, it is argued, has to suffer like us the experience of watching the present slip irretrievably into the past,

---

3. Newbigin here foreshadows his consistent rejection of the separation made in modernity between "facts" and "values" — as though "private beliefs" had no bearing on "public reality," or vice versa; as though, say, "the existence of God" were a matter of "individual taste." See especially *The Gospel in a Pluralist Society* (1989), chapter 3 ("Knowing and Believing"), for a demolition of the false dichotomy "science is what we all know, and religion is what some people believe."

and awaiting the still unknown future, then He is not perfect and omniscient. He is not the God of the ontological argument. Therefore, we must conceive God as simultaneously comprehending the whole of time within His understanding. This is what is meant by eternity — not an endless continuation of time, but a quality of being which transcends time altogether. This also is what is meant by eternal life as a possession of the Christian believer. For the Christian, insofar as he is united with God through Jesus, shares in some degree, and will ultimately share to the full, this divine life of super-temporality. He also comes to be able to transcend time. And it is from this circle of ideas that the eschatology which we have just criticized derives, that is to say, eschatology without a literal eschaton. Just as, in this view, we understand the word "everlasting," when used of God, to be not a literal attribution of endless temporal continuity, but a symbolic statement in terms of our time-conditioned experience, of a reality which transcends time altogether: so when we talk of the end of the world and the Day of Judgment, we are using temporal language as a symbol of a non-temporal reality — of the eternal and spiritual fact that at every moment God is equally present as judge and disposer of men's deeds. [Expand][4]

What are we to say, then, of this view? Is temporality to be predicated of God literally or symbolically? We are all aware that certain of the words we use about God are symbolic and not literal. When we speak of God's being Most High, we do not mean that He is removed a great distance from the earth's surface in the same way in which the top of Mount Everest is removed. We regard the spatial phrase as a pure symbol of something quite different, namely, God's moral and spiritual transcendence. On the other hand when the psalmist says, "Like as a father pitieth his children, so the Lord pitieth them that fear him," most Christians take this not symbolically but literally. That is to say, they regard God's love to men as being really what we understand by a father's love — though of course immeasurably more pure and good than the best parental love we know. That is to say, we take love when predicated

---

4. Newbigin frequently contrasted the ancient (Greek and Hindu) and the biblical views on the relation between God and time, or between God and the world. This contrast continues to be drawn from the study booklet *What Is the Gospel?* (Madras, 1942, p. 5) through the University of Chicago lecture of 1954 ("The Quest for Unity through Religion," in *The Journal of Religion* 35 [1955]: 17-33) to *Christ Our Eternal Contemporary* (Madras, 1968, chapter 2).

of God to be not something quite different from love as we know it, and only symbolically represented by the word love, but really and substantially love as we know it.

[The Thomist via media: analogy][5]

Now, when we speak of time in connection with God, are we speaking literally or symbolically? The Platonist (and the Hindu) answers unhesitatingly "symbolically." Space and time, he says, are both forms of purely human experience; and of both of them it is equally true that while we must use spatial and temporal language about God because it is the only language we have, we are to understand that it is symbolic.

[Support from Einstein — idea of time as a fourth dimension — this is very deceptive. Einstein shows that order in which events happen may be reversed in experience of observers. But they cannot be reversed in actuality.]

[Following Edwyn Bevan, two objections to this view seem to me decisive:

(a) We all believe that God can alter the future. Prayer. We do not believe that God can alter the past (Aquinas). It involves self-contradiction. Therefore past and future are radically different for God Himself.

(b) Time is fundamental to spiritual life as space is not. You cannot conceive spiritual life except in temporal terms. For example, repentance. After doing some wrong, you mentally turn away from it and try to set it right. After is not symbolic but literal. ("Turn away" is a term implying both spatial and temporal ideas: the spatial idea is symbolic, the temporal is literal.) If you reverse the temporal order — apologize first and do the evil deed afterwards — then the spiritual fact is different, not repentance but hypocrisy.][6]

We conclude that temporal language must be used in reference to God literally and not symbolically. But does this mean that this is a given fact for God in the same way as it is for us? We cannot say that, because that would make time, and not God, our ultimate. Time is the creation of God, but it is a real creation of which He takes account as He does of the rest of creation. If we hold fast to our fundamental faith

5. The interpretation of Aquinas on analogy is so contested that it would be foolhardy to hazard a guess at which line Newbigin followed.

6. The reference to Edwyn Bevan — who also deals with the false appeal to Einstein — will be to the chapter on "Time" in his Gifford Lectures of 1933-34, *Symbolism and Belief* (1938).

that the divine will is the only ultimate for thought, I do not think the problem is insoluble. Because it has pleased God to create this world and to make it the means of preparing a people for Himself, temporality, succession, has become a fact. For us it is a given fact over which we have no control, because it is simply the fact that God is — in our Lord's word — working. For God it is real, but it is ultimately subject to Him. We may conceive eternity as the completion of His work, when His purpose is accomplished, and succession is no more, and God rests. The word "rests" is symbolic insofar as it conveys the idea of fatigue and its cure, but it is intended literally insofar as it means the cessation of activity and the bringing into being of a condition of timeless bliss. We all know the story of the monk who wandered into the forest and, hearing the song of a bird, stood entranced to listen: when he returned to his monastery he found that he had been away a hundred years. We may take that as a parable of eternity — a condition of perfect enjoyment of the beauty of God in which all successiveness ceases because both God and also His creatures are at rest. Of this eternity the Sabbath is the perfect symbol. All that I am trying to say is contained in the Genesis story, which says that after God had worked, He rested. God is not only activity, as some have argued. When His work is done, He rests. His working is time — real for Him, but subject to Him; real for us and not subject to us. His rest is eternity.

This has important consequences for the Christian life. It dictates the conditions under which it can be said that eternal life is the present possession of the Christian. He does not possess eternal life by escaping into a condition of union with a God for whom time is unreal. He possesses eternal life by faith — which is the substance of things hoped for. His faith — his personal committal to and union with and love for God — enables him, as it were, to grasp in some degree already that goal to which God is working, and therefore to refresh his soul by it in anticipation. Insofar as he is united by faith with the will of God, he can in some sense share God's own vision of His perfect kingdom when the long travail of history shall be over, and in that vision he can rest his soul. Just as sympathy with the mind of a friend will enable us to grasp and share in his vision for the future, so that faith in God to which we have been won by his revelation of Himself in Christ enables us, however dimly, to see the goal and to rejoice in, and share in, its bliss because we have already in a measure the mind of God. The oft repeated phrase that in the

Christian life the Kingdom of God is already proleptically at work means just this: the prolepsis is not a metaphysical marvel like some recent so-called experiments with time. It is the self-communication of God's will, grasped by faith here and now, which enables us already to live in the light of its final goal. And that is the sense in which it is also true to say that for the Christian eternal life is a present possession. His fellowship with the God who works leads him into the secret of God's rest: and of that final perfect rest, each passing sabbath should be a foretaste.

II

Now a second objection to taking literally the New Testament eschatology, and it may be put in a variety of ways: "It is not necessary for the Christian view of life, that history should have a happy ending. We have now all that we ought to seek, and all that we can have. We have God's revelation of Himself in Christ: that is God's last word. We neither can, nor ought, to look for anything further. God has shown us His nature, which is perfect suffering love. Thereby He has shown us the terms on which we may live lives of victory and peace, even in the midst of the evil of the world. To ask for anything more is to show that one has not understood the gospel. In particular, the idea that whereas Christ came once in humility and obscurity to suffer for men, he will come again as a divine potentate armed with all the terrors of judgment, is a pagan idea which betrays the central Christian revelation. We ought not to ask for any better success than Christ had. What matters is not success, but faithfulness. We ought, as has been said, to perform all our duties in the spirit of a servant whose one concern is to carry out his master's will and who does not have the responsibility of worrying about his master's success or failure. Our only task is to be faithful, and to commit our work to God, our ever-present judge. That only is success and more than that we should not ask or expect."

What shall we say about this very plausible and popular line of thought?

First, I think it would have to be admitted that both the New Testament and the consensus of Christian opinion is against it. Hope has always been held to be a Christian virtue — one of the three abiding ones.

38

If we were to accept this view, we should have to write off hope not as a virtue but as a misunderstanding. I do not think that if hope were really removed, if you really convinced men that this life as we know it is really God's last word for the world and that there is nothing to look forward to, the resulting life would be recognizable as Christian at all. [Expand][7]

Second: we seem to have a similar error when it is said that faithfulness is itself the absolute good apart from the consideration as to the object of that faithfulness. A servant who faithfully serves the wicked or futile purposes of a bad man is not absolutely good: he ought to transfer his faithfulness to a cause which is good and efficient. In the same way we cannot discuss the question as to the objective results of God's purpose by saying that what matters is faithfulness since it is questionable

---

7. Hope was a recurrent theme in Newbigin's writings. Its absence was what struck him most on his final return to Britain in 1974. In *The Gospel in a Pluralist Society* (1989), when listing the characteristics of "the congregation as hermeneutic of the Gospel," he says this (p. 232):

> And finally it will be a community of hope. . . . One of the most striking features of contemporary Western culture is the virtual disappearance of hope. The nineteenth-century belief in progress no longer sustains us. There is widespread pessimism about the future of "Western" civilization. Many Christian writers speak of our culture in accents of embarrassment, guilt, and shame. In his study of contemporary Western society, the Chinese Christian writer Carver T. Wu finds as its two key elements "technological optimism and literary pessimism" (*Being and Relation: A Theological Critique of Western Dualism and Individualism*, p. 1). Technology continues to forge ahead with more and more brilliant achievements; but the novels, the drama, and the general literature of the West are full of nihilism and despair. It is not surprising that many Western people are drawn toward Eastern types of spirituality in which the struggle to achieve the purpose of a personal creator is replaced by the timeless peace of pantheistic mysticism. . . . The Gospel offers an understanding of the human situation which makes it possible to be filled with a hope which is both eager and patient even in the most hopeless situations. . . . It is only as we are truly "indwelling" the Gospel story, only as we are so deeply involved in the life of the community which is shaped by this story that it becomes our real "plausibility structure," that we are able steadily and confidently to live in this attitude of eager hope. Almost everything in the "plausibility structure" which is the habitation of our society seems to contradict this Christian hope. Everything suggests that it is absurd to believe that the true authority over all things is represented in a crucified man. No amount of brilliant argument can make it sound reasonable to the inhabitants of the reigning plausibility structure. That is why I am suggesting that the only possible hermeneutic of the Gospel is a congregation which believes it.

whether men can go on giving faithful service to something which is doomed to permanent and irremediable failure. It is certainly highly questionable whether man can give faithful service without taking an interest in the future of the cause he serves.

Third and more fundamentally, the view raises the whole question of the place of reward and punishment in the Christian life. It is the background of all moral questions that this world as we know it is characterized by the success of wrong values. What is evil succeeds, and is praised: what is good fails, and is censured. Consequently it is an elementary maxim of ethics that by seeking for the rewards and shunning the sufferings of the world, we shall not achieve virtue. But does this truth apply ultimately and finally? Is it true to the very end, finally, always, and without the possibility of any contrary appeal to God or anyone else, that goodness fails and evil succeeds? If it is true, is the moral struggle sustainable at all?

To answer that would of course itself require a course of lectures in ethics, but I will simply record my own personal convictions for what they are worth. I do not think the conflict between what is and what ought to be is spiritually bearable unless we believe that somehow, sometime, it is going to be resolved. And I think that the word "ought to be" has in it also, as an undertone of meaning, "ultimately shall be." I think if you take out that undertone of meaning, the word "ought to be" loses precisely that authority which is its distinctive quality. If a man says "ought to be but in fact isn't and never will be," I think we always know that he is preparing to surrender with a mere show of battle. Without this background of "in the end shall be," "ought to be" becomes a mere pathetic aspiration that everyone can safely ignore. It only derives its power from the implied assurance that though it is now not so, ultimately it will be.

If this be false; and if there is really no connection between ought to be and shall be; if, that is, there is no assurance that one day right values will be recognized for what they are and acknowledged: then there are consequences that we must face. One is — as I have said — that hope is not a virtue but a delusion. Another is that the pleasure we feel when real goodness is publicly acknowledged, or when a noble man's efforts are at last successful, and the disgust we feel when some plausible scoundrel wins for himself a reputation for sanctity, are both groundless and delusive feelings which ought to be banished. If the garland of success is a good thing, then we ought to be as glad to see it on the brow of a scoundrel as on that of a saint, for the idea that goodness and reward belong together is an illusion. Similarly if suffering be a good thing, we ought to be as glad to see an innocent man punished as a guilty one. Our feelings in both cases ought to be the same, and the supposed connection between evil and retribution ought not to bias our feelings.

I believe that once these logical implications are faced, it is not possible to doubt that the moral life requires the assurance that what "ought" to be, ultimately shall be. And "shall be" is a verb in the future tense which is meant literally and not symbolically. Let me put the same truth in a slightly different way. It is basic to all Christian ethics that the final judgment upon conduct is the judgment of God. All Christians would agree with that. Not the judgment of contemporaries, not our own judgment, not even the judgment of history so-called, but the judgment of God is that with which we finally have to deal. If we deny that, we have to say that in the end only results matter, and motives do not. This is what Marxists say, and they are logical about it. They know that it means throwing overboard the whole Christian moral tradition. But it is common, I think, to all Christians that the final judgment, and therefore the judgment with which we have to reckon, is the judgment of God.

Now what does this mean? It is a statement about present spiritual fact; thus far we can agree with Dodd. It is a fact relevant now at every moment. But is it only that? Look at the phrase "the final judgment": "final" is a temporal phrase; it means last of a series in time. To say that the final judgment is that of God is to say that at the end of the temporal process God will judge and that after that there will be no appeal. Now if this time reference is taken literally, it is understandable that the certainty of this future fact should become a factor in every present decision. In that sense judgment is a present spiritual reality: the eschaton is present in that sense, at every moment. But if we deny that "final" means, literally, at the end of the temporal series, I confess I do not see what kind of reality is left at all. We might believe that at every moment God, so to speak, mentally recorded His own perfectly just judgments upon all our motives and actions, but if that were all, we could neither take account of it, nor even know of it. A judge's own mental notes are not a judgment. A judgment occurs when the judge's conclusion about the case in question is given public effect, so that as far as possible "is" is made to correspond to "ought." If that does not happen, then the judge's mental notes are of no significance at all. In the same way I do not see how the vital truth of Christian ethics that God's judgment is the final judgment can have any validity at all, unless it be true that the end of the time process is an effective judgment by God, in which, by virtue of His justice and His power as creator, right values are vindicated and wrong values condemned, and the dichotomy between what is and what ought to be is finally ended.

Fourth: What shall we say of the view that since Christ's revelation of God is final, we ought not to expect or hope for anything further, or anything different? Once more this is a question whose proper answering would require a whole course of lectures on the meaning of the Atonement. Only a very brief expression of personal opinion is possible.

Beneath the view we are combating, there lies the implication that in Christ and His revelation the idea of divine punishment or retribution is superseded. In the cross, it is sometimes said, it is revealed that God, instead of punishing sin, Himself bears it. I am sure this is a disastrous mistake. What is revealed in the cross is this piercing paradox that God who punished sin and will punish sin Himself bears the punishment, and thereby it is made possible for the sinner to repent and turn to God in faith. So far from superseding the idea of divine punishment, the cross itself requires it. The piercing quality of what happened on Calvary is that the Son of God died the death proper to a criminal. If it had been that He died for men only in the sense that a scientist who gives his life in dangerous medical research dies for men, the death of Jesus would have been quite other in its meaning from what it is. What is central is that the kind of death which we instinctively feel to be proper to the most brutal and callous murderer was suffered by the sinless and spotless Son of God. It is that that assures us that the very depths have been plumbed for us by God's love. But if we are to believe that the whole idea of punishment as proper to evil is an illusion, then our central feeling about the cross is also an illusion. If the connection between sin and suffering is illusory, we ought to feel the same about Jesus on His cross as we do about the foulest criminal on his; the fact that we feel differently is because we know that one deserves it and the other does not. But that statement implies that there is a proper and necessary connection between sin and suffering, and it is precisely that necessary connection which the view we are considering denies. Thus this view ultimately robs the cross itself of its real significance.

We know that sin and suffering belong together, not as an accident, but by a necessary connection. They ought to belong together — and that is another way of saying that God punishes sin. That is not an Old Testament doctrine abrogated by the gospel. It is taught by Jesus in the Gospels with an absoluteness that is nowhere exceeded in the Old Testament. But it is just because we know and cannot escape from that fundamental certainty, that the cross is what it is to us, the demonstration that the God against whom we have sinned and who rightly punishes sin, Himself drinks to the very dregs, deeper than even the foulest sinner has to drink, the cup of punishment. The paradox reaches its climax when He whom we know as the Word made flesh cries out "My God, My God, why hast thou forsaken me?" God bereft of God that He might save those who have sinned against God. I know it is sheer paradox, but I firmly believe that the heart of the gospel is there, and that if you remove one side of the paradox, and say that in the cross belief in divine punishment was shown to be an error, I think you both undercut all real moral experience and also take the power out of the cross itself.

If this be so, then Paul Tillich is right when he calls the death of Christ not the eschaton, but the center of history. It is final in the sense that God has there revealed the very depths of His heart: we cannot ask for a further revelation of His will. [Expand][8] But it is not final in the sense of being the culmination of the working of that will. That culmination, the true eschaton, is still future. And we can and must look forward to it in hope.

III

I pass to a very brief consideration of a third form of the objection to this New Testament eschatology. It may be put something like this: "The idea of an actual end of history followed by a divine judgment seems to be inconsistent with the thought of God's perfection in the fol-

---

8. Newbigin seems to have had in mind Paul Tillich's *The Interpretation of History* (1936), part 4, section 2 ("The Interpretation of History and the Idea of Christ"). Tillich there says, in various slightly different formulations, that "for Christian thought, Christ is the center of history in which beginning and end, meaning and purpose of history are constituted" (p. 251) — albeit I cannot find any reference there to the death of Christ in particular.

lowing way. It implies that at a certain point in the ever-developing time process He decides, as it were, to stop the loom and take a pair of shears and cut right across the texture of human history. What matter whether some souls have not yet reached perfection? What matter that all kinds of promising possibilities are cut off unfulfilled? At that arbitrary point history is to be cut off, and some of God's children to be written off finally as failures and only some accepted as fit for the new age. Does not this mean, therefore, that God has partially failed in His purpose? And is not such a doctrine inconsistent with belief in the perfection of God's love and power?"

What say?

First: It implies a view of history as a continual developing process. Hence the sense of arbitrariness at this process suddenly being arrested. But we have already seen reason to think that this view of history is false. We have accepted rather the view that history is a growth of good and evil side by side, a real growth of good — a real attainment of progressively higher goods, but along with this an equally real growth of evil — a growth in the power and range of evil forces. If this be the true view of history, then a catastrophic eschaton might not be arbitrary but necessary. We know how within history itself we see evil forces growing, organizing themselves with greater and greater power until they overshadow the whole world and men begin to ask whether there is a God in heaven at all — but when the moment comes, these forces are utterly destroyed. May that not be a microcosm of history itself? May it not be that the time will come when the long struggle of good and evil can lead no further and the final overthrow of evil and the consummation of all the long travail of goodness becomes necessary? If this be the true reading of history, then the consummation of God's purpose, as it has been grasped and served by faithful men in all ages, can only come by the destruction of evil and the cosmic renewal such as the New Testament envisages. That would be not an arbitrary interruption of the slow and painful growth of goodness, but its only true fruition.

Second: We have here to face the questions of whether belief in God's perfection requires us to believe in universal salvation, or whether it is possible that even in the end some of God's children may finally be lost, and to that extent God's purpose partially fails. There is no subject about which it is harder to speak, yet there are some things which it seems to me we have to face. We do know that Christ spoke of

44

an unforgivable sin. We do know as a matter of spiritual fact that it does sometimes happen that by refusing God's love and hardening his heart, a man sinks progressively deeper into sin with every fresh revelation of that love. That seems to be part of the implications of human freedom, and we do not know of any means by which God can certainly prevent it. I do not see how, once we have granted the fact that this is so, we can theoretically deny the possibility that it may continue to be so. The settled direction of some human souls does seem to be downwards, and even the revelation of God's love on the cross only seems to accelerate that movement. There is no more awful fact in the universe, but it is a fact. And I do not find anything in the Gospels to contradict it.

Two things of a constructive kind may, I think, be said; firstly this, that whatever that dreadful day may bring further, it will be not arbitrary but right. The whole meaning of the doctrine is that right is to be done, and right is what we learn of our Lord Jesus, when we commit ourselves wholly to Him. Whatever may happen in the final judgment, it can only be the confirmation of what is revealed to our consciences in the gospel about the nature of the spiritual world. And secondly this, that the only right way to think about this matter is to think about it in relation to oneself. This is because the final judgment is a wholly inward judgment, and we do not wholly know the inner heart of any other. But as we allow our hearts and consciences to be illuminated by the revelation of God's love in Jesus, and as we cleanse them, by the daily discipline of honesty, from all subterfuge and self-deception, I think two things steadily become clearer to our minds: one is that I myself deserve only condemnation because in the bottom of my heart there is still an unsurrendered egotism that over and again flouts God's love and breaks His laws. The other is that God's forgiving love to me in Christ is a sheer marvel that passes all comprehension. These two certainties grow together in the soul. They are the counterpart of that paradoxical duality in the New Testament language about God — His wrath and His love. Only where we understand His wrath, do we understand the might of His love. It is as we understand His love that we know that His wrath is just. Growth in Christ is a growth of which that tension is the true growing point: as love — the real love that is caught from Calvary, grows in strength, it reveals itself as big enough to contain wrath too. Such love alone is redemptive, because it is an echo of the mighty, wrathful, pardoning, suffering love of God Himself.

Lecture IV

What has gone before has been mainly cast in the form of criticism, which is notoriously a much easier task than construction. But in the course of what has been said, I trust that certain broad positive suggestions have become clear. I have tried to suggest a picture of what seems to me the right kind of eschatological hope. In the center of the picture is the hope of a new world, a re-created universe in which the travail of history shall find its completion and its rest. That, I have suggested, is the true object of hope. It remains to try to show in one or two directions what is implied in that picture and to inquire how far it meets the problems which were the starting point of our inquiry.

I

We will take first of all the third of what I called the cardinal points of New Testament eschatology — the doctrine that death and resurrection are the connective terms between this present life and the re-created life of the new age.

Between us and the Kingdom of God as a fully realized fact lies death. It cannot but be so. We saw before that the idea of a perfect society under conditions of mortality is impossible. The perfect society cannot lie this side of death. And moreover it cannot be the direct result of our efforts. We all rightly shrink from the phrase "building the Kingdom of God" not because the Kingdom does not call for our labor, but because we know that the best work of our hands and brains is too much marred by egotism and pride and impure ambition to be itself fit

46

for the Kingdom. All our social institutions, even the very best that have been produced under Christian influence, have still the taint of sin about them. By their own horizontal development they cannot, as it were, become the Kingdom of God. There is no straight line of development from here to the Kingdom.

The outward attestation of that spiritual conviction is the fact of death. Across our path this obliterating shadow lies: not only must we, body, mind and spirit, personality as a whole, go out into the dark unknown, but also all our labors, our achievements in science, in art, in social and political progress — all is destined sometime to be swept away and forgotten. Everything in the end, even if that end be the promised death of the solar system, is destined to be buried in the dust of failure and death.

Our faith as Christians is that just as God raised up Jesus from the dead, so will He raise up us from the dead. And that just as all that Jesus had done in the days of His flesh seemed on Easter Saturday to be buried in final failure and oblivion, yet was by God's power raised to new life and power again, so all the faithful labor of God's servants which time seems to bury in the dust of failure, will be raised up, will be found to be there, transfigured, in the new Kingdom. Every faithful act of service, every honest labor to make the world a better place, which seemed to have been forever lost and forgotten in the rubble of history, will be seen on that day to have contributed to the perfect fellowship of God's Kingdom. As Christ, who committed Himself to God and was faithful even when all ended in utter failure and rejection, was by God raised up so that all that He had done was found to be not lost, but alive and powerful, so all who have committed their work in faithfulness to God will be by Him raised up to share in the new age, and will find that their labor was not lost, but that it has found its place in the completed Kingdom.

For this the fifteenth chapter of 1 Corinthians is our guide. In this chapter the apostle assures the Corinthians that as Christ has been raised — the first fruits — so shall they that are Christ's be raised at His coming. For as in Adam all die — as death is the hallmark of the natural humanity which we all share: so in Christ shall all be made alive — this new life is the heritage of all who are in Christ. Then after some verses about the second coming of Christ, he goes on to deal with a question: "How are the dead raised, and with what manner of body do they come?" He answers with the analogy of a grain of wheat. The grain falls into the ground and appears to be lost and dead. Out of it God raises up something new, not a mere extension of the grain, yet also not absolutely disconnected from it. It is only a rough analogy as the rest of the chapter shows. But the central idea is clear. "It is sown in corruption; it is raised in incorruption: it is sown in dishonor; it is raised in glory: it is sown in weakness; it is raised in power. It is sown a natural body, it is raised a spiritual body." Paul's conception of the future is not a disembodied survival: that is what he calls nakedness in 2 Corinthians 4. It is resurrection and re-creation — the creation of a new organism fitted to be the vehicle of perfect life. It is life raised out of death, a new life raised by the miracle of God's power out of the wreckage of all human hope and effort. And yet it is not utterly disconnected from what went before. It is we who are raised up, and transfigured. Of this we can only say, as Paul says, that it is a miracle for which we have no grounds of belief unless it be a fact that Christ was so raised from the dead. But if that be a fact, we have grounds for belief. Apart from that fact death is an impenetrable mystery, a gulf which no human thought can cross. Even we who believe in the resurrection of Jesus cannot build a bridge of logical thought across the gulf, and say "here and here is discontinuity; here and here is continuity." It is a mystery; but in the fact of Christ's resurrection we have our ground of belief that out of the ruin and corruption of death, God is able to raise His people, giving them a body as it pleases Him.

II

This doctrine of resurrection is the counterpart, on the personal side, of the doctrine of cosmic renewal. Resurrection is to a new life in a perfected society. [Expand][1] One of the starting points of our study was the

---

1. We may surmise that the expansion will have anticipated the last chapter of Newbigin's *Sin and Salvation,* which includes the following passages (pp. 122-25):

> The whole Body of Christ is one fellowship, and the whole body shall at the end be raised up to share in the glory which the disciples saw in the risen body of Jesus. . . . This new creation involves not only our souls and bodies, it also involves the whole created world. None of God's creation is irrelevant to His purpose. None of it is mere scaffolding to be thrown away when the building is complete. He made it

difficulty of seeing the right relation between God's purpose for the individual soul and God's purpose in history as a whole. Now these two are perfectly reconcilable if the aim of history is the creation of a perfect fellowship. For the only full fruition for the individual soul is in fellowship, and a perfect fellowship itself implies perfect souls who form it. Man is, we know, made for true community, and without it there is no fullness of spiritual stature for him. Therefore our difficulty was not any intrinsic incompatibility between personal perfection and social perfection. The difficulty arises from the fact of death. For death removes every individual abruptly out of history, before history has reached its goal of perfect fellowship, which is also the proper goal of individual growth. Death thus creates for each man the dilemma which was our starting point. It makes it impossible that his participation in the task of creating a perfect fellowship should lead him personally to his own perfection. Therefore the hope of finding his own perfection in an otherworldly heaven becomes a rival in his mind to the desire to labor for that perfect fellowship on earth which he knows he cannot see. We have seen that neither of these two rival ideas is by itself satisfying.

How does it come about that death thus bars the straight road to the Kingdom of God and creates this impossible dilemma for the man who seeks it? It is not an accident. As I said a few minutes ago, we cannot help connecting it with the fact of sin. It is due to the fact that, along with our quest for perfection, there exists, as a dark irrational mystery, all kinds of desires for things which are not perfection; the fact that, along with eagerness for the Kingdom, there is also a sheer unwillingness to surrender ourselves wholly to the King. It is because of this, I say, that the straight road to the Kingdom as fully realized fact is barred. Man's life is not just a striving for the perfect society; it is also a striving after other ends. Therefore man's striving cannot and does not lead in a straight line to the full realization of the Kingdom. Death, failure, corruption, bar the way. And hence arises that tragic dilemma when a man seems forced to choose between seeking the perfect goal of history

---

all in love, and He loves it all. Therefore the completion of His purposes means not only the resurrection, but also a new heaven and a new earth. . . . [The consummation] is the restoration of creation to its original purpose by the purging away of sin. It is the restoring of all men and all things to perfect harmony and perfect joy, through the perfect love of God.

which he will never see, and seeking perfection for himself in an individual survival of death. Both ways, as we have seen, are blind alleys.

It is when we stand face-to-face with this riddle that we understand St. Paul's words to the Corinthians: "Flesh and blood cannot inherit the Kingdom of God, neither doth corruption inherit incorruption (that way is barred). But when this corruptible shall have put on incorruption and this mortal shall have put on immortality, then is come to pass the saying that is written: Death is swallowed up in victory. O death, where is thy sting? O grave, where is thy victory? The sting of death is sin and the power of sin is the law, but thanks be to God which giveth us the victory through our Lord Jesus Christ" (cf. 1 Cor. 15:50, 54-57).

Christ gives us the victory because He has broken the power of sin, and in breaking the power of sin, He has broken the power of death. Death is still a fact. In Adam all die. The barrier is still there. What we are assured of in Christ is that death is not the last word, but that God in His mercy is able out of the ruin of corruption and death of men and of man's social institutions to raise up that perfect incorruptible society which is our true goal. It is the assurance that that goal *is* in the end to be reached — though we cannot reach it in a straight line by our own power.

That perfect society, the fully accepted and accomplished rule of God in men's hearts, therefore is the object of a Christian's hope and longing. And he knows that even though he himself must go out into the darkness of death, and that even though all his efforts for the creation of a better society on earth must in the end be buried and forgotten, yet none of this is lost. In that day it will all be found to be there raised up, transfigured. It will be seen that all the labors of faithful souls to create true human fellowship have been not lost, but taken up and consummated in the perfection of God's Kingdom. That is the proper object of hope. Whoever is faithfully seeking — whether as an engineer, an economist, a politician, a craftsman, a teacher, or a friend — to overcome that which militates against true human fellowship and to create such fellowship in great ways or in small, may be assured that even though all the visible results of his labor perish before his eyes, it is no more lost than is he himself if he dies in faith. The outward implements of fellowship will perish; but in the day when the perfected people of God are gathered together in the fellowship of the Kingdom, he will know that his work was not in vain.

III

This conception of the goal of history settles the nature of all Christian action in the world. We have already seen reason to reject the idea that Christian action is to be conceived of as "building the Kingdom of God." Flesh and blood cannot inherit the Kingdom of God. Does that mean, then, that the Kingdom does not summon us to action at all? If the full realization of the Kingdom of God is purely God's act, do we have simply to await it passively? That is a conclusion no one could accept. But on the other hand, if all human effort is destined eventually to end in failure as far as worldly effectiveness is concerned, do we need to bother about our actions? What is the true relation of Christian action to the coming of the Kingdom?

I believe that the right answer is given in Albert Schweitzer's phrase, that Christian action is a prayer for the coming of the Kingdom.[2] Let me explain. I have urged that the final fulfillment of God's Kingdom is to be understood as a cosmic renewal, including resurrection, of all faithful service that has been buried in defeat and death. And we have agreed that our action cannot lead directly in a straight line to that fulfillment. But Christian action, done as in the sight of God, for His sake, acknowledging that He alone is final judge, and that the Kingdom must be His gift — such action is a kind of prayer offered to God that He may hasten His Kingdom. It is a prayer that He can and will answer, because it is one where praying itself makes us and the world more fit to receive the answer. It is action done in hope of God's Kingdom and directly committed to God. I think we have the same view of Christian action in St. Paul's words near the end of his life, "I know Him whom I have believed, and am persuaded that He is able to keep that which I have committed unto Him against that day" (2 Tim. 1:12). The

---

2. Newbigin was fond of citing such a dictum of Albert Schweitzer; it occurs at several points in his later writings, though always without further reference. The closest I have been able to track down is a passage in Schweitzer's *Christianity and the Religions of the World* (1923), which includes the following sentences: "Jesus does not speak of the Kingdom of God as of something that comes into existence in the world and through a development of human society, but as of something which is brought about by God when He transforms this imperfect world into a perfect one. In the thought of Jesus, *the ethical activity of man is only like a powerful prayer to God, that He may cause the Kingdom to appear without delay*" (pp. 32-33, emphasis added).

apostle's life of ceaseless labor, sometimes successful, sometimes not, sometimes successful for a time and then apparently undone again by the folly of others — all this had been something committed to God. It had been a sort of acted prayer. And because he knew the God to whom he had committed all this, he knew that it would not be lost whatever happened, but would be kept against that day when it would find its consummation in the New Jerusalem.

One objection may still perhaps be waged against this view of Christian action. It may still be felt that it does not satisfy our longing to have part in a great purpose which really and visibly leads to a goal: "The thrill of being part of a great movement of progress and of seeing its ends realized, is something necessary for social action. And if we are to accept your view, the end seems to be so disconnected from the beginning as quite to rob us of that sense. The end can hardly be said to be the *result* of the beginning at all, and therefore it does not satisfy the longing we have to take part in a real progressive movement and to see results."

I think this objection ought not to detain us. When it is examined, it is found to rest upon motives which are in the last resort egotistical. It means really this: "We want to be able to identify ourselves with a movement of social progress, and to see it succeed, so that at the end we can say 'we have succeeded' and indeed 'I have succeeded.'" I do not think we can deny that this egotistical element does play a part, sometimes a distressingly prominent part, in progressive social action. The enthusiast, instead of identifying himself with the cause and keeping his eyes fixed on its purpose, identifies the cause with himself, and thinks only of its success in terms of *his* success. We all know that kind of enthusiasm. But it is just this for which the view of Christian action leaves no place. It invites a man to long for and pray for the goal, and to make his prayer articulate in work. And it offers him the certainty that in the end the goal will be realized. But at the same time it makes it quite clear to him that when that blessed hour comes, he will have to say not "*I* have succeeded," but "God's will has been fulfilled. Thanks be to God."

These then are the motives of Christian action. A Christian is one who, through Christ, has been reconciled with God who is the King. God's rule is operative in his heart, through gratitude to Christ. If God so loved us, we also ought to love one another. His gratitude impels him to acts of love towards men, but he also acts in hope — hope of the final completion of God's Kingdom in a perfected fellowship. Even though his actions may all seem to be failures as far as visible effectiveness is concerned, he commits them to God as his thank offering, in the sure hope that they will not be lost. And by faith, the substance of things hoped for, he now possesses in his heart a foretaste of the joy of that perfected Kingdom in which God's purpose shall be complete.

If these are the underlying motives, what sort of criteria do they furnish, especially for Christian actions in the larger matters of society?

IV

I have already said that I believe that the greater part of the problems facing humanity today are problems calling for political solutions. The technical conditions of modern life, the means by which commodities are produced, distributed, and sold, are such that the individual alone is almost powerless to alter his lot. As an individual he feels himself to be, and is, a helpless speck in the vast, semi-automatic, impersonal machinery of life. A large part of the attraction of totalitarian philosophies of life has been the fact that they have shown themselves able to take hold of and control these anonymous economic forces in the name of certain easily understandable ends such as national aggrandizement, and so have given to their adherents the sense that they were in control of the machine, and not merely controlled by it.

This being the case, I do not see how the Christian can avoid concerning himself with politics. Love to men, and the fundamental obligation to seek everywhere to create true fellowship, cannot be made effective except over a very small range of life, without invoking political means. To forswear politics means surrendering control of 75 percent of life to forces over which neither the Christian, nor anyone else, has any control. That cannot be called a serious attempt to implement the requirements of God's rule.

Political action means action in relation to and in collaboration with large bodies of people. Otherwise it is not effective political action. Politics never allows us to choose exactly our own way, but compels us to decide between a very small number of politically possible alternatives. This means, therefore, that Christians taking part in politics always find themselves working with people who are not Christians and do not share their motives or their ultimate aims. It is this that creates the extreme tension which is always involved in Christian political action. That tension cannot be avoided.

It seems to me, in the light of what has been said, that in his political and social action the Christian will exercise his influence rather against the tendency to exercise the imagination in making blueprints of a new and perfect world order, and in favor of efforts of a humbler kind to deal concretely with existing evils and put them right. His realism about the nature of history as a concomitant growth of good and evil will prepare him on the one hand for the necessity, in due time and place, of using force against those who selfishly resist the common will in the name of private rights; he will not imagine that his program will be carried through simply by the force of its own reasonableness. On the other hand, the same realism will prevent him from supposing that if only the existing world order can be demolished and a new and rational one imposed in its place, the real problems of human life will be solved. He will know that each advance will bring with it fresh problems, but he will, it seems to me, exercise his influence in favor of tackling and removing actual evils as and when it becomes possible, rather than in favor of utopian dreams.[3]

He will know also, I think, that while political action is obligatory, it is not the only means, and probably not the most fundamental means, by which society will be changed. I think it is historically true that the biggest social consequences of Christianity have originated in movements which did not begin by aiming at social reform at all. [John Wesley][4]

But this is in no way a belittling of the necessity of political action. If we neglect political action when we have the opportunity of it, then we stultify the religious movement itself because we fail to implement

3. The tone of "realism" in this passage is probably indebted to Reinhold Niebuhr's *The Nature and Destiny of Man* (1941-43), the first part of which Newbigin had heard as the Gifford Lectures at the University of Edinburgh in the spring of 1939. By the time of the second series, given in the autumn of that year when the war with Hitler's Germany had already begun, Newbigin was sailing back to India, where he had to remain for the duration.

4. Much has been written on the effects, direct and indirect, of Wesley and Methodism on English society, albeit the thesis of Halévy that England was thereby spared a "French revolution" is no longer fashionable.

the commandment of love to neighbor. If the men who came out of the Evangelical Movement — men like Shaftesbury and Wilberforce at one end, and the early leaders of the Trades Union and Co-operative movements at the other — had shrunk from political and social action when it was possible to them, it would not be possible now to speak of the Evangelical Revival as having transformed English social life.

[A point which is relevant to our work in India — General Booth][5]

The fact that most of our work is concerning the lowest strata of society, who are at present largely politically powerless, ought not to make us feel that our chances of influencing Indian society as a whole are small. Rather it seems to me that the reverse is true. Insofar as we can do for the outcaste villages of India what John Wesley did for the downtrodden laboring classes in Britain, we shall ultimately transform India as surely as his movement transformed Britain.

But the point is that that is not our goal, great as that is. If transformation of Britain had been Wesley's goal, he would never have achieved it. Our goal is the holy city, the New Jerusalem, a perfect fellowship in which God reigns in every heart, and His children rejoice together in His love and joy. To that we look forward with sure hope, and for its sake we offer up to God all that we do in response to His invitation to love our neighbor as we ourselves have been loved. And though we know that we must grow old and die, that our labors, even if they succeed for a time, will in the end be buried in the dust of time, and that along with the painfully won achievements of goodness, there are mounting seemingly irresistible forces of evil, yet we are not dismayed. We do not need to take refuge in any comfortable illusions. We know that these things must be. But we know that as surely as Christ was raised from the dead, so surely shall there be a new heaven and a new earth wherein dwells righteousness.

And having this knowledge we ought as Christians to be the strength of every good movement of political and social effort, because we have no need either of blind optimism or of despair.

---

5. The reference is to General William Booth (1829-1912), founder of the Salvation Army.

THE HENRY MARTYN LECTURES

Delivered in the University of Cambridge
1986

I. Authority, Dogma, and Dialogue

It is surely very proper — meet, right, and our bounden duty — that this University should honor the memory of Henry Martyn, who devoted his brilliant intellectual gifts to the effort to communicate the gospel to the people, especially to the Muslims, of India and what was then called Persia. From his ordination at the age of 24 to serve as curate to Charles Simeon, here in Cambridge, to his death at Tokat in Armenia at the age of 31, he blazed like a brilliant star, and burned himself out for the sake of the gospel. He translated the New Testament into Urdu, Arabic, and Persian, and his translation is still the basis of the present Urdu New Testament. Moreover, any history of the rise of the modern ecumenical movement must include the fact that it was in Henry Martyn's house on the banks of the Hooghly in the first decades of the nineteenth century that Anglicans, Baptists, and Congregationalists met regularly for prayer, that William Carey outlined to the others his project for a decennial world conference of missionaries of all denominations, the first to be held at the Cape of Good Hope in 1810, and that in Henry Martyn's words, there was "a union of hearts unknown between persons of different denominations in England."

Brother Carey's pleasing Bengali dream was realized only a hundred years later, and this University again had an important part in that achievement. It was in 1882, following a visit by Dwight L. Moody, that seven of the most outstanding athletes in the University volunteered for foreign missionary service. The men of the Cambridge Seven electrified the British universities, and this was the spark that ignited the Student Volunteer Missionary Union which took as its slogan "The Evangelization of the World in this Generation." That in its turn, under God's providence, led the way to what William Temple in his enthronement sermon at Canterbury in 1942 called "the great new fact of our time." He was referring, of course, not to the ecumenical movement itself but to that which makes it possible, namely, the fact that the church was now for the first time in its history a worldwide communion. That great new fact was, in and under God, the fruit of the missionary experience in which Henry Martyn was one of the earliest pioneers, and the Cambridge Seven among the most notable representatives. It was the outcome of that period which Kenneth Scott Latourette in his eight-volume history of the expansion of Christianity calls "The Great Century."

And it is a thrilling story. My own conversion to the Christian faith as an undergraduate here fifty-seven years ago was entirely bound up with the vision of the gospel as a reality which embraced the whole world, offered for the world. At that time it did not seem odd or eccentric to be headed for missionary service. The question asked was not: "Why be a foreign missionary?" It was rather: "Why not?"

Today the situation is very different. As a nation, we have turned in upon ourselves, and as churches, we are much less confident about the gospel. From both points of view, the foreign missionary enterprise is seen as a very ambivalent affair. We may admire the heroism of Henry Martyn burning himself out in seven short years of passionate effort to communicate the gospel across the barriers of language, race, creed, and culture, but we are frankly embarrassed about the foreign missionary enterprise as a whole. The missionaries of the great century are accused, by Christians as well as others, of arrogance, of ignorance of the riches of other faiths and other cultures, and of reliance on the advantage which European military and economic power gave them, even when they went in the name of the crucified Jesus. To put it bluntly, was this great missionary expansion so intimately bound up with the imperial expansion of the Western powers that the former was really nothing but the religious aspect of the latter?

Plainly there is truth in this charge. It would be foolish to deny it. But it would be foolish also to pretend that it is the whole truth. While there have been and are times when the expansion of Christianity goes against the currents of political power — as in the first three centuries, or more recently during the cultural revolution in China — there have also been long periods when the currents went together. The prestige of Rome, for example, certainly had something to do with the conversion of the barbarian tribes of western and northern Europe. No one would now say, however, that the one was just the religious aspect of the other.

We are living through the collapse of our modern Western culture, or at least the collapse of confidence in it, if indeed they are not the same thing. We find it easy to accuse our grandparents of the blunders implied in bracketing Christianity with what they called civilization, so that missions were hailed as the bearers of Christian civilization. The same people who make these accusations are often singularly blind to the fact that the modern term "development" is no less laden with the unexamined assumption of a culture about what is needed for a good life. Our judgments are often anachronistic. When we read of David Livingstone's ambition to open up Africa for the gospel and legitimate commerce, we judge him in the context of the multinational corporations which have entered the doors he opened there, and not in the context of the slave trade which he was laboring to expose and to displace. It is easier to repent of the sins of our grandparents than to recognize and acknowledge our own.

But the low esteem into which foreign missions have fallen is not to be understood simply as the result of the guilty conscience of that somewhat bedraggled species, the White Anglo-Saxon Protestant. That is an important part of the explanation, but not the whole of it. Even in situations where the old colonial pattern has completely disappeared and there is no suggestion of cultural imperialism, there is in the churches, I submit, a widespread feeling that it is improper to claim that the gospel is the unique and decisive offer of salvation to all humanity. In situations such as the one where I now work — the inner city area of Birmingham, where Hindus, Muslims, and Sikhs form a majority of the population and Christians are a minority, a situation in which there can be no imperialist overtones in the approach of Christians to their neighbors of other faiths — one finds among Christians a real embarrassment about commending the gospel as the way of salvation. Indian Christians, accustomed to a more robust approach to their Hindu neighbors in India, are astonished at what seems to them the timidity of English Christians. They may be naïve in their judgment, but they are right in detecting among Christian natives of this country a widespread feeling which may be expressed in two statements:

1. There is the feeling that it is arrogant to suppose that we have the truth and must simply tell it to others and expect them to accept it.
2. This is particularly true in the field of interfaith relations because the other religions already have so much that is worthy of respect and even of veneration that the arrogance of the missionary is particularly offensive.

I am deliberately using vague language to try to express what I think are widely shared feelings. To examine what is involved in these will be the business of the first lecture.

I

I begin with the first and more general view, which regards with suspicion any confident assertion of the truth in matters of religion. The use of the adjective "dogmatic" to condemn such assertions provides a convenient introduction to the discussion. Dogma, deriving from the Greek *dokein,* meaning "to seem," is a word used to denote that which seemed good to a competent authority and is so promulgated. It is so used of the apostolic decrees in Acts 16:4. More generally in the history of the church it has been used to denote that which has been authoritatively given and is to be received in faith. It was so understood for many centuries. In our contemporary culture, by contrast, the readiness to question dogma is regarded as one of the marks of intellectual and spiritual maturity.

Now it is beyond question, however we may evaluate it, that Christianity began with the proclamation of something authoritatively given. Paul always presents himself not as the teacher of a new theology but as the messenger commissioned to announce a new fact — namely, that in the ministry, death, and resurrection of Jesus, God has acted decisively to reveal and effect His purpose for the whole world. Obviously the New Testament writers understand this fact in different ways. But it is one set of facts which they are interpreting, the facts concerning Jesus, and they are at one in regarding these as of decisive importance for all people.

The proclamation invites belief. It is not something the truth of which can be demonstrated by reference to human experience in general. It calls for acceptance by faith. It rests on no authority beyond itself. When challenged for their authority, its representatives can only reply: "in the name of Jesus." But it is set forth as the truth, not as one possible opinion among others. And of course it can be rejected, and it is. The New Testament repeatedly affirms a radical contradiction between the apostolic message and the wisdom of the world. The affirmation of this contradiction reaches its terrifying climax in the Johannine accounts of the arguments between Jesus and the authorities of His own people. But it is implicit from the beginning in the opening call of Jesus to repent, to be converted, to turn around and face in the opposite direction, as the necessary condition for being able to believe the gospel, that is to say, to believe that the Kingdom of God has now become a present reality.

However grievously the church may have distorted and misused the concept of dogma in its history, and indeed it has done so grievously, the reality which this word tries to express is present from the beginning and is intrinsic to the gospel. Something is given which cannot be demonstrated from the general truths of experience and reason available to all people. It is a new fact to be accepted by faith, a gift of grace. And what is given claims to be not just a possible opinion but the truth. It is the rock which either will be the rock on which one builds, or the stone on which one stumbles and falls to disaster. Those who — through no wit or virtue of their own — have been entrusted with this message cannot demonstrate its truth; they can only live it and announce it.

As I said earlier, to be able to subject such a dogmatic affirmation to critical questioning is — in our culture, as in the culture which Paul encountered in Athens — the mark of a mature person. Perhaps our culture has prided itself more than any other on its readiness fearlessly to question any dogma, however ancient and venerable. It is therefore natural that the missionary, with his confident announcement of a message which he claims to be *the* truth for everyone, should be an object of suspicion. Is he not simply a naïve survivor from a pre-critical age? Must we not all accept that truth is much larger, richer, more complex, than any one culture, let alone any one mind, can grasp? Is it not more fitting, more honest as well as more humble, to offer whatever contribution we may think we have to the common human search, to enrich it perhaps, but not to take it over? Is it not fitting that we abandon the role of missionary with a truth to proclaim, and humbly accept the role of fellow searchers for the truth along with all people of good will?

To this it seems to me that three comments are in order. First, the opinion that doubt is more intellectually respectable than belief is merely one of the prejudices of our culture; it rests upon a confusion of thought. It is, one might say, a dogma which will not stand up under critical scrutiny. For a little reflection will show that all doubt rests upon implicit belief. We can only doubt a proposition on the basis of what we find more worthy of belief, and we can only affirm that a proposition is not proven if we believe that there are relevant criteria for proof. No doubt is possible except on the ground of beliefs which we have to hold in order to be able to doubt.

Secondly, we need to attend to what we have learned from the sociologists of knowledge about what Peter Berger calls "plausibility structures." Every society depends for its existence on patterns of accepted beliefs and practice which determine which beliefs are plausible to members of that society and which are not. These plausibility structures are of course different at different times and places. Thus when, in any society, a belief is held to be reasonable, this is a judgment made on the basis of the accepted plausibility structure. In discussions about the authority of the gospel, the word "reason" is often used as though it were an independent principle of authority to be set alongside revelation and tradition. But clearly this is a confusion of categories. Reason does not operate in a vacuum. The power of a human mind to think rationally is only developed in a tradition which itself depends upon the experience of previous generations. The definition of what seems reasonable and what does not will be conditioned by the tradition within which the question is being asked. Within an intellectual tradition dominated by the methods of the natural sciences, it will appear unreasonable to explain things in terms of the exercise of personal will, of purpose. But if God exists, and if He is capable of revealing His purpose to human beings, then the human reason will be required to understand and respond to the revelation and to relate it to other experience. But it will always do this within a tradition which determines whether or not any belief is plausible, in this case the tradition of the community which cherishes and lives by the story of the revealing acts of God.

It is no secret that the gospel offers a radically different vision of how things are from that which shapes all human societies. The church, as the bearer of the gospel, therefore inhabits a plausibility structure at variance with those which control all human cultures, and it is hard to call them into question.

Third, there is an admirable air of humility about the statement that the truth is much greater than anyone can grasp, but it can be very deceptive when it is used to neutralize any confident affirmation of the truth. How does the speaker know that the truth is so much greater than this particular statement of it? What privileged access to reality does he have? In the famous Indian story — often quoted in this context — of the blind men and the elephant, the whole point of the story is that the king and his courtiers can see that it is an elephant while the blind men are only groping after parts of the truth. The story is usually told in order to suggest that a proper humility will refrain from confident affirming "this is the truth." In fact, however, the story embodies an immensely arrogant claim to know the reality after which the great world religions are only groping. As Polanyi has trenchantly put it: "The emphatic admission of our fallibility only serves to reaffirm our claim to a fictitious standard of intellectual integrity hidebound in contrast to the attitude of those who openly profess their beliefs as their final personal commitment." [The reference is to Polanyi's book *Personal Knowledge*, p. 271.]

To go into all the world with the affirmation that God has revealed and effected His purpose of love for all people in Jesus Christ is not arrogance. It is not imperialism. It is the necessary sharing of what we have been given, and to withhold it is not merely disobedience and ingratitude to our Savior: it is also betrayal of the trust placed in us for the sake of all those who share our common humanity.

II

But to say this does not settle the question how the Christian affirmation is related to other affirmations about ultimate truth, and it requires us to consider the relation of the Christian affirmation to the affirmations made in the name of the great world religions that God has revealed Himself in other ways than in Jesus Christ. The debate on this question is voluminous and often passionate. In contemporary English theology the predominant opinion is against making the kind of exclusive claims for the Christian gospel that have been part of missionary thinking during the great expansion of the past two centuries.

A lucid and well-balanced contribution to the debate has recently been made by the Indian Roman Catholic theologian Gavin D'Costa in his book *Theology and Religious Pluralism* (1986). He identifies three types of answer to the basic question, naming them pluralist, exclusivist, and inclusivist. For the three positions he takes respectively John Hick, Hendrik Kraemer, and Karl Rahner as key figures. His final vote is for the third of these. Recognizing that such typologies can never do full justice to the views of every contributor, one nevertheless provisionally accept the classification as a useful way into the discussion. All three are Christian positions, claiming fidelity to the gospel. All seek to relate faith and the universal scope of God's saving purpose, on the one hand, to the centrality and decisiveness of Jesus as Savior, on the other. The starting point of the pluralist's position, as stated by Hick, is the universal salvific will of God. On this premise Hick feels bound to conclude that all will ultimately be saved, including those who never had any contact with the Christian religion. It follows further that God's saving will is also operative in the non-Christian religions, and indeed within systems of thought which make no religious claim but are capable of turning people from self-centeredness to Reality-centeredness. When the argument is stretched — as Hick does stretch it — to include non-theistic and even atheistic systems of belief among the agents of God's saving will, one is bound to ask whether the Reality which is the true center of all beliefs of whatever kind is not an entity about which we have to be totally agnostic. If it truly answers to every conception which people have formed of it, there is in fact nothing that we can say about it except the *neti neti* of the Upanishads: not this, not this. From where then does Hick gain his assurance that the reality of which nothing can be certainly known is in fact a universal salvific will? The answer is quite clear: it is from Hick's own encounter with Jesus, of which he speaks movingly in many passages. However radically he may try to demythologize the Incarnation, it remains true for Hick that God's character and will are disclosed in Jesus. It is here that he finds the certainty of a universal saving purpose.

Consequently, Hick's "Copernican revolution," as he calls it, cannot be carried through. It is in fact logically impossible. It is of course true that God, and not any of the religions, is the central reality. But we have no standpoint from which we can observe the identity or difference between God as He really is and God as He is conceived in the world religions, including our own. For if I speak of "God as He really is," I am working with a concept of God which has come to me through my nurture in one of the religious traditions of the human race — unless, indeed, I am speaking of the wholly unknowable, and in that case I ought not to speak at all. I certainly cannot speak of a universal saving will.

D'Costa next turns to Kraemer as representing what he calls the exclusivist position. Central to this position is the uniqueness and decisiveness of what God has done in Jesus Christ. Kraemer draws a sharp contrast between this and all of the world's religions, including Christianity. While God does make Himself known in nature and history and in the religious consciousness which all human beings share, the religions as such are misdirected forms of the human search for God, in no way to be compared with God's unique action in Christ for the salvation of the world.

The heart of D'Costa's critique of Kraemer is that his position is internally inconsistent. If God is as He is revealed in Christ, then He must be willing the salvation of all. It is inconceivable that He should consign to perdition the nations who have not heard of Jesus, including the saints of the Old Testament who lived before the Incarnation. In other words, if God's act in Jesus Christ is normative, it cannot be exclusive. D'Costa complains that Kraemer treats the religions too schematically as monolithic entities whereas they are in fact multifaceted and in constant change and development. And while Kraemer is right to distinguish the gospel as the record of God's saving action from Christianity as one among the world's religions, it is wrong to say, as Kraemer seems to do, that the gospel and Christianity can be understood in isolation from each other. As a good Catholic, D'Costa sees — rightly I believe — that the church is part of the gospel.

It is the inclusivist position, particularly as expounded by Karl Rahner, that D'Costa finds acceptable as embodying the truth in the pluralist and exclusivist positions while avoiding their errors. In other words, the inclusivist position does justice to the two fundamental Christian affirmations, that God wills the salvation of all, and that salvation is offered in Jesus Christ mediated through the church. Jesus Christ, the Incarnate Son of the Father, is the decisive and normative revelation of God. All questions about God are to be answered by reference to Him. Christ's presence now is mediated through the church, and therefore Christianity is the absolute religion for all people. But while the revelation in Christ is normative, it is not exclusive. God's grace is universally active, and all true human living is a response to grace. Until the coming of the gospel to any people, other religions — among them the religion of Israel — are lawful. They are means through which grace is mediated, for, since we are social beings, there is no mediation of grace except through such social entities. The religion of Israel, for example, before the coming of Christ, provided the means by which they reached salvation. Thus the adherents of the non-Christian religions are to be regarded as "anonymous Christians," since they already have a measure of grace and grace is always the grace of God in Christ. But from the moment that the gospel reaches them and is truly presented to them, the anonymous must become explicit. It must find fulfillment in the church, since one who thus explicitly accepts Christianity has — to quote Rahner — "a still greater chance of salvation than someone who is merely an anonymous Christian" (D'Costa, p. 88). If the explicit acceptance is withheld, the religion is no longer lawful and the person is no longer an anonymous Christian. The church is thus not the exclusive company of the saved, but the sign of a salvation offered to all but still hidden in those not yet its members. To quote D'Costa's summary, "The grace that is operative within the non-Christian seeks its correct objectification, through its dynamic orientation, in Christ and the Christian Church" (D'Costa, pp. 107-8). Here is the raison d'être of the church's mission to the nations.

It is clear that each of the three positions has its strengths and its weaknesses. Hick's position is grounded in his own personal experience of the overflowing goodness of God as he has met it in Jesus Christ, and that leads him to his confidence that such a loving purpose must in the end prevail. That is a profoundly Christian position. But when Hick tries to detach it from its Christian origin and — for the sake of universality — deny any uniqueness and finality to the gospel, he ends up with something that is hard to distinguish from the monism of the Vedanta, in which ultimate reality is Nirvana, without character, unknowable and unknown.

The strength of Kraemer's position lies in his insistence upon the uniqueness of those events which are the subject of the gospel. They are — as Kraemer always insists — *sui generis.* I cannot follow D'Costa in his repeated attack on Kraemer's use of the phrase. If he says, as he repeatedly does, that Kraemer is wrong in regarding the gospel events as *sui generis*, D'Costa is under obligation to point to something else which is really of the same kind — not a myth or story, not a concept or doctrine, not a philosophy, but a series of events within secular history which can be compared with the events which we relate when we spread the gospel. Of course there are the nature myths of dying and rising gods; there are the stories of the many avatars of Vishnu. These do not pretend to refer to events in secular history to which a date and place could be assigned. The events concerning Jesus Christ are, I submit, unique, *sui generis.*

However, D'Costa is right in some of his criticism of Kraemer. Kraemer does fail, I think, to recognize that you cannot make an absolute separation between the gospel and the community which, from the beginning, is the bearer of the gospel both in preaching it and in seeking to live by it. Here Rahner is right in his insistence that gospel and church cannot be separated — though they can and must be distinguished more clearly than Rahner perhaps would allow. But D'Costa is wrong in assuming — because of Kraemer's insistence on the uniqueness of the event of Jesus Christ as providing a way where there was no way between sinful man and holy God — that all who have not explicitly confessed Christ as Savior are in Kraemer's view lost. He takes this also to be Barth's position. Clearly as regards Barth he is wrong. Indeed conservative evangelicals have accused Barth of universalism, and they have some grounds. But as far as I can see, Kraemer did not attempt to answer the question about the ultimate fate of unbelievers. D'Costa holds this against him, as do Rahner and the other Roman Catholic writers. As I shall say later, I think there are good evangelical grounds for Kraemer's silence at this point, but certainly the question is bound to be asked: If Jesus Christ is God's unique and decisive way for sinful men and women to come to God, what is the fate of those who refuse it?

The inclusivist position seeks to do justice to both the basic affirmations of the Christian faith: the universality of God's saving will, and the uniqueness and decisiveness of Christ. There is much in Rahner's statement which must be wholeheartedly accepted: that all human life is lived under the grace of God whose lovingkindness is over all His works; that Jesus Christ as the Incarnate Son of God is truly the One by whom we must measure all that claims to be of God; and that the message of salvation through Christ cannot be separated from the church which is the bearer of that message — all this is truly affirmed in the inclusivist position.

My difficulties with the inclusivist position can be indicated in a series of questions. First: Does Christianity really provide the explicit manifestation of that which is present in a hidden and anonymous form in the non-Christian religions? The idea of Christianity as the fulfillment of Hinduism was ably presented by J. N. Farquhar eighty years ago but it had to be abandoned. It did not correspond to the facts. At many points Christianity, rather than being "The Crown of Hinduism," contradicts its strongest affirmations, or answers questions which Hinduism does not ask; and this is even more obviously the case if we consider Islam.

Second: If the fulfillment model is the true one, why is it that the most devout and truly godly among non-Christians often oppose the preaching of the gospel most passionately? Why is it that from the time of the New Testament until today, the godly and the devout reject Jesus, and the people outside the pale of the higher religions are the ones who eagerly follow Him? Why should even a devout and sincere inquirer like Nicodemus be told that he needs a total rebirth, if he is to enter the Kingdom?

And why, thirdly, is it in the religions that we are to find anonymous Christianity? Rahner is right to say that all human beings live by God's grace, and he is right to say that because we are social beings God's grace reaches us through social entities by participation in which we live a human life. But why does he go on to conclude from this that grace must be made available through, and not despite, the non-Christian religions? (D'Costa, pp. 85-86). Why the religions? Why not other forms of human society through which we receive the kindness of God — family, nation, sports club, trade union, university, or whatever? What reason is there for supposing that organized religion is the sphere in which grace operates? There is much evidence to suggest the contrary. The prologue to the Fourth Gospel, which contains the classic statement of the universality of God's life-giving grace, tells us that the light shines on everyone, but it shines in darkness — and the subsequent story shows that it is religion which is, above all, the area of darkness.

This brings me to the fourth question to be put to the inclusivist. Rahner supports his thesis about the role of non-Christian religions in mediating the grace of God by reference to the religion of Israel. He treats this as one of the non-Christian religions and argues that, until the coming of Christ, it was the lawful religion for the people of Israel and was, to quote D'Costa, "the concrete means by which many attain to salvation" (D'Costa, p. 86). This surely illustrates the confusion created by taking the "religions" as a class into which Christianity, Judaism, Islam, Hinduism, Buddhism, etc. can be placed. This whole way of talking presupposes a standpoint outside of any of the ultimate faith commitments which these names stand for. It would be simply incomprehensible for any New Testament writer to treat Christianity and Israel as two alternative religions. The Bible of Israel is also the Bible of the church. And quite explicitly, the New Testament, while affirming the place of the saints of Israel in the company of those who are on the way to salvation, also affirms that they without us could not be made perfect (Heb. 11:40). Salvation for Abraham and Moses and Gideon and Baruch, as for Peter and Paul and John, is still in the future.

This final comment on the inclusivist position provides a point of entry for an evaluation of the whole debate which I would like to attempt. The point, the crucial point it seems to me, is the concept of salvation. In this whole discussion which I have so briefly reviewed, there is an unexamined assumption that we know what we are talking about when we ask such questions as: Will the devout Hindu or Muslim be saved? It is the unexamined concept of salvation which needs to be scrutinized. The whole discussion, if I am not mistaken, is focused on the destiny of the individual's soul after death. But that is not at all the focus of attention in the Bible. Attention is focused on the final event in which God will complete His purpose for all humankind and all creation. The urgent question is not: How shall I be saved? But: How shall God's name be hallowed, His Kingdom come, His will be done on earth as in heaven? The focus is on knowing and doing the truth now, so that we may be partakers of the corporate and cosmic consummation at the end. Not only in the Old Testament but also in the New, the commanding vision is not of a way by which I can leave this world for another where I shall be safe, but of the way by which God will come to this world, the way by which God will come to this world to communicate His purpose for the whole creation. Salvation lies in the future for Abraham and Moses and David as much as for me. And being saved means being made part of the company which bears in its life and communicates to the world the secret of what God has in store for His whole creation. Rahner therefore is right in saying that the church is part of the gospel and that the church is not the exclusive company of those who have an entrance ticket for heaven, but the sign to the world of a universal salvific purpose — sign, and I would add, foretaste and instrument. But he is surely wrong to see the world religions as the agencies through which grace is mediated apart from the church. We must not identify the working of God's grace with the presence of religion. Wherever there is kindness, goodness, faithfulness, truthfulness, there the grace of God is at work and everyone who loves God will acknowledge it, welcome it, rejoice in it — whether it be found in a religious person or a person of no religion.

I want to affirm with Kraemer the unique and decisive character of God's action in Jesus Christ, and I want to insist on Kraemer's favorite phrase to describe it: it is *sui generis.* It is not to be understood as one of a class: it is unique. But I want to protect this affirmation against the assumption which is often made, that this implies necessarily the ultimate perdition of those who have not explicitly accepted Jesus as Savior. D'Costa assumes that this is what Kraemer's position involves; and if Kraemer himself was silent on the point, D'Costa, with others, takes it that Kraemer was insufficiently rigorous in developing his beliefs. I do not believe that this is so. As I find myself in D'Costa's book classified as an exclusivist, I will try to say why.

I think all reasonable people must agree that if God had so ordered things that our final weal or woe was determined by the accident that some missionary had or had not brought the story of Jesus to my people; if the consequences of such a defect (whether or not the missionary were to blame) was the eternal perdition of whole peoples — this would be irreconcilable with the revelation of God's universal saving love in Christ Jesus.

This is an argument from within the Christian faith. It is not obvious that God is a loving Father who purposes the salvation of all His children. It is not a conclusion that can be drawn from observation of all the facts. The facts, taken as a whole, provide massive evidence to the contrary. If we believe it, it is because of what we understand of the gospel.

Reasoning, then, from what God has done in Christ, we affirm — rightly I believe — that God wills the salvation of all. It is the next step which is crucial. How does God will to accomplish it? The inclusivist assumes that for those who have not yet had an opportunity to meet the church and hear the gospel, God must will to accomplish it through the religious consciousness which is common to humankind and which finds its expression in the world religions. The exclusivist says God wills to accomplish it through the witness of the church to the gospel, but the final accomplishment of God's will can only be at the end, which is the end for all humanity together, and for all creation. And, I would add — if I am so classified — that this exclusivist will insist that the explicit teaching of Jesus forbids us to suppose that I know in advance who are the saved and who are the lost; warns me that that day will be a day of surprises; summons me to remember that if I have been called to be a disciple of Jesus, it is not just for the sake of my salvation but that I may be a witness to the world; informs me that it is I who must live in the awareness that there is a fearful judgment awaiting the unfaithful steward.

The crucial issue in this debate centers, I think, in the doctrine of election, a doctrine which is hardly touched in D'Costa's discussion, but which is fundamental to any biblical doctrine of mission. If salvation is understood in individualistic terms, as it so often is in this discussion; in other words, if the central question is, what is going to happen to each individual soul when it departs this earthly life: then the idea that this will be settled by an accident of history unrelated to the faith, devotion, and virtue of that soul is intolerable. But, as I have said, this does not seem to be the central concern of the Bible. That concern is with the ultimate manifestation of God's glory in a redeemed creation and a redeemed humanity. None will share that glory until it embraces all for whom it is intended. Since, therefore, humanity is seen as a whole, as one family with whom God has made His covenant of blessing in Noah, it follows that God's saving purpose is effected not by a separate dispensation for each individual but by a dispensation which binds the human race and all its history into one. This is the logic of election. One is chosen in order to bring the good news of salvation to others, one people for all the peoples. We are thus bound to one another in that very act by which we are taken up into God's saving action. Salvation is an action of God which binds together those who share in it. If there is one Name given for our salvation; if there is one society bearing the power of that Name to all the nations to the end of history, that is because humanity is one family and salvation can only be the restoration of an original unity in the one final consummation. That is why the church is sent to all the nations bearing the one Name.

Israel has been chosen for the sake of the nations. But Israel has rejected the Messiah. Why? In order, says Paul in Romans 11, that the gospel may go to the Gentiles, so that in the end Israel too may receive it as a gift from them — always from one to others. So the fullness of the Gentiles will be gathered in, and all Israel will be saved — even unbelieving Israel! Shall we call this pluralist, exclusivist, or inclusivist? It is none of these. It is working with a quite different picture of salvation. Salvation is corporate and eschatological. Plainly millions of Jews have died as unbelievers, yet Paul says "all Israel shall be saved." It is not, as Rahner says, that Jewish religion apart from Christ was the means of salvation until Christ came, and then ceased to be so. Paul believes in the ultimate salvation of Israel in spite of unbelief. For Paul, as for the rest of the New Testament, the congregation of Israel in the Old Testament *is* the church of God. Like the whole church before and after the Incarnation of the Son of God, it looks towards a salvation yet to be revealed. That is the day when final judgment will be given. Till then believers must beware of supposing that they have an advantage over others. "If God did not spare the natural branches, neither will He spare you." So "be not proud, but stand in awe."

This picture of the matter does not correspond to any of the three models which D'Costa defines as pluralist, exclusivist, and inclusivist. In spite of the charge made by Rahner and others that this is an evasion, I want to insist that to concentrate so much attention on the question, "What is the fate of unbelievers?" is to abandon the spirit of the Scriptures. We have news to share, good news beyond all we can imagine. It is not the offer of a secure place in heaven for ourselves to the exclusion of others. The moment we think of it that way we are — as Paul warns us — in danger of being cut off. The action of God in Christ, into which we are brought by the Spirit in the fellowship of the church, gives us both the clue to find our way through the darkness and complexity of this life (which is the only life we know) and the power of love to sustain us through all its conflicts. We cannot keep this to ourselves. To refuse to share it is to contradict and strangle it. But we know that we always, with all others, are still *in via*. We have not arrived. We do not possess the truth. We are learners. And if one thing is made clear in the teaching of Jesus, it is that at the end we shall be surprised. The first will be last and the last first. The one who thought he had a claim to a place in the house will be left outside and the rank outsider will be in. Therefore our Lord refuses to speculate with His disciples about how many will be saved but simply tells them: you try to find the narrow door. Therefore Paul says, judge nothing before the time. And therefore also we must reject the complaint of those who say we are not responsible theologians if we answer the question about the fate of unbelievers by simply saying, "They are in the hands of One who is both more holy and more merciful than we are." That is the only proper answer.

What, then, does this imply for our understanding of interfaith dialogue? Dialogue has become a blessed word which evokes images felt to be more humble, more authentic, than the traditional image of the missionary preaching to the heathen. Dialogue suggests a readiness to listen and to learn, to sit where they sit and share insight and experience, in contrast to the monologue of the preacher who stands while they sit and proclaims while they listen. These contrasted pictures prompt two initial reflections. First: whether we like it or not, preaching in its original sense of announcing a forthcoming event, telling good news, is and has been from the beginning part of the Christian style. Jesus preached. Paul stood up in the Areopagus and preached to the Athenians. If you have important news to tell about a forthcoming event, you have to tell it. It will not emerge in the course of conversation.

But of course conversation follows. All missionaries have been involved in conversation and were certainly total failures if they were not. But they did not usually dignify this with the name of dialogue. I have recently been reading the delightful reminiscences of a former colleague — E. O. Shaw — with whom I shared the work of village missionary. He writes about conversations with Hindus in the temple, in the street, walking in the country, as a guest in Hindu homes. His heart is warmed by the good things in the life of simple Indian farmers and shopkeepers which these conversations bring to light. And quite naturally he talks about Jesus and shares with his friends something of the gospel. These are ordinary human conversations, and they are the stuff of missionary life.

And not only of the life of people set apart for a special calling as missionaries. Most of the worldwide spread of Christianity has been the result of millions of conversations of this kind carried on by ordinary people in the course of ordinary daily life. What presuppositions make such a conversation possible? Not, surely, that I the Christian am saved, but my partner in conversation is lost until I can, somehow, through the conversation, bring him to accept Jesus as Lord. How could any ordinary human conversation take place on that basis? And yet even in the inclusivist position as outlined by Karl Rahner, that would be the situation.

What kind of conversation is possible on the basis of a pluralist position? Here it is taken for granted that Christianity is among a number of approaches to the truth, that it is not to be presented as *the* truth, but is a contribution to the shared quest for a truth which is beyond us all. This is, not infrequently, what interfaith dialogue is thought to be. But the quest for truth is not serious unless there is at least a provisional commitment to some clues, some pointers, some kinds of evidence which can be accepted. In a real living conversation between people who are not merely dabbling in debate but are seriously concerned to find the way through life's complexities, the participants will try to convince their partners of the truth as they see it, or at least of the value of the clues they are following. If we are to speak at all about God and His purposes, we have to commit ourselves to some affirmations about what we believe to be true, and to seek to share our perceptions with our partners, because truth which is merely private and personal is not truth.

What are the presuppositions of a truly missionary dialogue? Certainly a Christian cannot accept as the presupposition of dialogue that God's revelation of Himself in Jesus Christ is less than, or other than, the truth; that there is accessible to us a revelation of God which relativizes that which is given in Jesus. The Christian is one who has been laid hold of by Jesus and called to follow Him. But he does not pretend to have the fullness of truth, to possess it; he is a learner on the way, but he knows the way even though he does not see or possess the goal. He can seek because he has been found. Believing that Jesus is the way into the fullness of the truth, he will be ready to open himself to all reality from whatever side it comes and to grasp all new truths in the power of the Truth which has grasped him. This involves risk. There is no true dialogue without risk. A person whose mind is incapable of being changed is incapable of genuine dialogue. To refuse the risk, to refuse the encounter of other perceptions of truth is implicitly to deny that Jesus is the way, the One through whom we are enabled to come to truth in its fullness.

This way, the way of discipleship, is a way of action and not only of thought. The way in which we are invited to walk is one of active obedience. Therefore I think that the most fruitful kind of interfaith dialogue is one in which people of different faiths or ideologies, who share a common situation and are seeking to meet ordinary human needs, are enabled to share the insights which their different beliefs give them for contemporary action. It is in this situation of active discipleship, where we cannot take refuge in established formulations of doctrine but have to probe new and unexplored territory, that we learn what it means to trust Jesus as the way, the truth, and the life, and as the One who can lead us into the truth in all its fullness.

Dialogues, conversations, sharing in discussions, which means both talking and listening — all this is not a new replacement for traditional mission. It is, always has been, and always must be an integral part of mission. We are called both to preach and to listen, and our preaching will be a mere beating of the air if we are not listening. But, we have good news to tell, a gospel to proclaim. It is entrusted to us. If we fail to proclaim it, we are unfaithful stewards. It is not for one nation or race or culture. There is something quite intolerable about the idea that Christianity is the proper religion for the European races, but that for the others, other faiths are proper. My Indian Christian friends in Birmingham sometimes meet this attitude among English Christians, some English clergymen, and find it deeply offensive. What God has done in the incarnation, death, and resurrection of Jesus is no private affair for a few. It is God's decisive action for His whole family and for His whole creation. It is for all the nations. We cannot be silent when such a tremendous secret has been entrusted to us. We have to tell the world. That was true when Henry Martyn left Cambridge for India. It is true now.

II. Conversion, Colonies, and Culture

The story of Jesus as it is given to us in the Gospels begins with a call to conversion and ends with the commissioning of the apostles to go and make disciples of all nations. How are we to understand this call to conversion, and how are we to interpret it as it bears upon the many and varied cultures of humankind — of the nations? Is it true, as is often said, that in the attempt to carry out this commission, in calling the peoples of many nations to be converted, missionaries have ignored or despised the rich cultures which these peoples had developed over many centuries? That, by persuading them that their culture was part of the sinful world from which they had to turn, the missionaries have destroyed precious things which they did not understand and created in effect colonial enclaves dominated by the culture of the missionary? What is the relation between the call to conversion and the authenticity of culture?

The first preaching of the gospel is at the same time a call to conversion. "The Kingdom of God is at hand: repent and believe the Gospel." That is the good news, the thing which has to be told. It can be told but it will not be believed except as the result of a radical reorientation of mind and will. "Repent, turn around, be converted, and believe what is being told — the good news." The call is literally for a changed mind. It is as though one were to say: "Turn around and look in a different direction. You are looking the wrong way. What you think the rule of God will be is not what it is. If you are to grasp it at all, you will have to do a complete U-turn." This is not just the familiar cry of the prophets: "Return to Yahweh!" It is not the preaching of revival in the sense of return to the old faith. Nor is it, as the Good News Bible has it: "Turn away

78

from your sins," since that would imply that the hearers already know what are sins and what are not. The whole point of the story as it unfolds is that we do not. The so-called sinners are the ones who believe, and the so-called righteous are the ones who are unable to believe. The Fourth Gospel develops the theme with relentless insistence. The divine presence overturns the world's conceptions of sin, of righteousness, and of judgment. Without a radical change of mind, the presence of the Kingdom is simply hidden. It cannot be discerned. Faith is not a possibility for the human heart except for those to whom God Himself gives it. For the rest, the parables become mere riddles, and the mighty works become occasions for stumbling, and are attributed to the devil. And finally, in the experience of the early church, the affirmation that the cross is the manifestation of God's wisdom and power, of the presence of the Kingdom, is in the eyes of the world scandal and folly. The call to conversion is so radical that it seems to suggest a total break, a complete discontinuity between the old and the new, between the world and the church, between the children of darkness and the children of light. Although it is the Fourth Gospel which takes this theme to the limit, an attentive reading of the synoptic gospels gives plenty of evidence of the sharpness, the radicalness, of the call. Indeed, in every strand of the New Testament evidence it is made clear that to follow Jesus means to accept the way of the cross — that most potent symbol of absolute rejection by the world.

What I have been saying — and I have been trying faithfully to represent the teaching of the New Testament — suggests a total discontinuity between the gospel and the life of people apart from the gospel, a total discontinuity between gospel and culture. The long-running debate which followed the publication of Kraemer's book on "The Christian Message in a Non-Christian World" centered around the words continuity and discontinuity. Karl Barth, with his rejection of the idea of "points of contact" for the gospel in the non-Christian religions, appeared sometimes at least to see only total discontinuity. But of course there cannot be a total discontinuity. If there were, there would be no way of communicating the gospel, for the communication has to use the language of the people to whom it is addressed. That language is shaped by and embodies a way of understanding the world. It is itself the heart of a culture. The gospel may call — does call — for a radically new way of thinking about God. Yet the Bible cannot be translated into any language without using the words of that language to translate *Theos* and *Kurios,* and the words used will have to be the words which take their connotations entirely from a pre-Christian concept of divinity and of lordship. There is no escape from this necessity. The radical break will come when, through the actual encounter with the words and deeds of Jesus, a wholly new understanding of what the word "God" means, of who God is, breaks in.

And it does — as the experience of countless Christians from all the cultures of the world bears witness. If one asks such converts to say how they understand the continuity and discontinuity between their life before and after conversion, the answer — I think — is likely to be somewhat as follows. The preaching of the gospel is seen as a threat to one's accepted tradition of belief, something to be resisted. But in the life of the Christian after conversion, it is possible to look back and value things that were there before but are now seen in a different light. To Saul the Pharisee, Jesus can only appear as an enemy, a subverter of the law, and in the name of the law he must be resisted. To Paul the Christian the law can be seen as a divinely provided guardian to lead him to Christ at a time when he could not yet know Him. There is perhaps a parallel here to the "paradigm shifts" which Thomas Kuhn has described in his survey of the nature of scientific revolutions. There is no logical argument by which one can move from Newton's physics to Einstein's; from the point of view of Newton's universe, Einstein does not make sense. But in Einstein's universe, Newton's laws can be seen to be true of large bodies moving at speeds far from the speed of light. Seen from one side, there is discontinuity; from the other, continuity. I am only suggesting an analogy, but I think it is helpful and corresponds to the experience of many converts who have followed the steps of Paul.

However, as long as we live in the world, the tension between gospel and culture remains. The gospel is always culturally embodied because it refers to the Word made flesh, to the involvement of the divine in human history. If I, using the English language, affirm the gospel, its most basic form will be the sentence "Jesus is Lord"; the question immediately poses itself: What, in English culture, does the word "lord" mean? What is "lordship" in this culture? At once a whole set of images suggest themselves, images which my Christian discipleship requires me to reject. To the end of my life — apart from contact with any other culture — I shall be both tempted to interpret Jesus' lordship in the terms suggested by my culture and at the same time challenged to re-think my inherited ideas of lordship after the patterns of lordship manifested in the Jesus of the Gospels. There is no such thing as the gospel pure and simple. Every statement of the gospel, and every exercise in the living out of the gospel, is culturally conditioned. And yet the gospel exercises and will always exercise a critical function within any culture in which it plays a part.

What then are the issues involved in the *cross-cultural* communication of the gospel — the communication of the gospel by people of one culture to people of another? What does it mean "to disciple the nations" — if we understand "the nations," as we must do, not as the two hundred or so nation states which presently belong to the United Nations Organization, but as all the culturally distinguishable groups which make up the human family?

I

The simplest and most natural answer to the question is that discipling means "making them like us." Missionary history furnishes an abundant stock of stories, many would say horror stories, to illustrate this way of interpreting the missionary task. But we would miss the point if, in our present mood of embarrassment about nineteenth-century values, we confined our attention to recent history. It seems clear from the New Testament that the first disciples also saw the matter in this way. "It is necessary," said these godly men who formed the core of the original church in Jerusalem, surveying the motley crowd of pagans whom Paul had attracted in the cities of Galatia: "It is necessary to circumcise them and charge them to keep the law of Moses." What could be more obvious? The law was a hedge protecting an oasis of godliness in a world full of uncleanness. Israel was the garden which Yahweh had planted, watered, pruned, and nourished through the centuries. The mission of Jesus had been in the first instance to Israel. He had himself been circumcised and had never called in question the fundamental mark of the identity of God's chosen nation. He had certainly reinterpreted the Sabbath law, but always on the basis of the truer reading of the law itself. What more natural, then, that Peter should resist the suggestion that he should compromise himself as a loyal Israelite by accepting the hospitality of an uncircumcised pagan soldier? The writer of Acts sees the experience of Peter in the house of Cornelius as a decisive turning point in the story of the church's mission to the nations. What resulted from that event was not that Cornelius and his household were added to a church which remained unchanged in its essential nature. It was not that a pagan family was brought out of the jungle into the garden. It was that a sovereign action of the Holy Spirit changed both Cornelius and Peter, both a pagan family and, when the Jerusalem church had grasped the message, the church as a whole. What was clear from that moment was that discipling the nations did not mean turning them into Jewish proselytes; it meant the coming into being of a new kind of humanity for which a new name had to be found — a Gentile Israel, people who were part of the one household worshiping the God of Abraham, Isaac, and Jacob, brothers and sisters of circumcised Israelites, and yet culturally still Gentiles, part of the heathen world, the nations. It surely needed amazing courage on the part of those devout Jewish disciples of Jesus to recognize that "discipling the nations" did not mean simply adding new members to the household of Israel, but that it would mean invoking the mighty power of the Holy Spirit to create something new, overturning old classifications, proving the world wrong in its fundamental ideas about sin and righteousness and judgment, leading the church into truth which could not even be glimpsed by the first disciples who accompanied Jesus in the days of His flesh.

It has been hard to remain faithful to that early lesson, to distinguish between proselytism — which is the exercise of a human agency drawing people into conformity with an existing style of corporate living and thinking — and evangelism, which recognizes the sovereign freedom of the Holy Spirit to make the preaching of Christ the occasion for doing a new thing, for taking all that belongs to the Father beyond the present experience of the church and so showing it to the church that the church is led into the fullness of the truth about Jesus, a fullness which is beyond the capacity of one culture or one generation to grasp. In a memorable sentence, the fifth assembly of the World Council of Churches at Nairobi in 1975 affirmed that Christ does not make carbon copies but originals. The charge is made against missions that they have tried to make carbon copies of European and American Christianity.

No one can deny that there is truth in the charge. However, the charge is often made with a naïveté which ignores essential factors in-

volved in the meeting of cultures. No living culture is static or monolithic. In all cultures there are tensions between conservatives and radicals, between the older generation and the younger. All cultures are —
even in the remote jungles of the Amazon Basin — exposed to contact
with other cultures. Contact with another culture may heighten the
tensions in society; the strange culture repels the conservatives and attracts the radicals just because it is different. There is an instructive
contrast between the attitudes of the anthropologist and the missionary
to the cultures they have encountered. One definition of an anthropologist is that he or she is a radical in his own culture and a conservative in
the culture which he studies. Because he is radical in his own culture,
traditional culture of another people is exciting and attractive just because it is new for him. But for the young radicals in the culture he studies, the traditional culture is boringly familiar, while the culture which
the anthropologist brings but which he finds boring, is attractive. In
each case what repels the one attracts the other. The missionaries of the
nineteenth century were probably in general conservatives in their own
cultures (not by any means politically conservative, but culturally conservative). Inevitably the gospel which they brought was expressed in
terms of their culture; it could not be otherwise. As such it proved attractive to elements in the receptor culture which were — for one reason or another — in rebellion against their traditional culture, either
because they were marginalized like the Harijans or Dalits in India, or
because they were young, the students who eagerly flocked to mission
schools and colleges. In many cases, the foreign culture was attractive
just because it was foreign. So the young people of Europe and America
who were rejecting traditional Western culture emphasized their rejection by putting on Indian clothes and chanting Sanskrit mantras. The
adoption of the outward marks of foreignness helps them to make their
point better, perhaps, than if they wore lounge suits and sang Hindu po-
etry to traditional English hymn tunes. One does not have to wear saf-
fron robes in order to believe the teaching of the Upanishads, but perhaps it helps to make the point.

Western Christians today, themselves embarrassed about the manifest evils of Western culture, are offended when they see Christians in
Asia and Africa clinging to the outward forms. Missionaries in India
have, in some places, succeeded in building churches modeled on a
Hindu temple — usually in the teeth of fierce opposition of local Chris-

tians. The extreme form of this insistence that Christians of other cultures should not be acculturated into Western cultural forms but should remain within their own culture is the program of separate development, usually known by its Afrikaans name *apartheid*. Merely to pronounce that name is enough to make the point that it is as wrong to absolutize culture as to ignore it. And the whole discussion leads us back to the central point, which is that conversion is a work of the Holy Spirit, and that where the Spirit of the Lord is, there is liberty — liberty to seize the opportunities offered by a new culture: freedom to maintain the old, freedom to experiment with different cultural forms in the continuing exercise of discipleship. If a culture is not free to change, it is dead.

II

If we must, then, reject the idea that "discipling the nations" means making them like us, we must also, I think, reject a move in the opposite direction, a move which would completely sever the link between conversion and cultural change. I am thinking here of Dr. Donald McGavran and the "Church Growth" school of missiology which he has so successfully fathered. As a missionary in India, Dr. McGavran was impressed by the fact that the work of different missions among the same people could produce such diverse results. In one place, the church grew rapidly; in another, it remained stagnant. On the one hand were people's movements in which the gospel was so accepted that it became part of a folk culture. On the other hand, McGavran saw the traditional mission station with its apparatus of schools, colleges, hospitals, technical colleges — locking great resources of money and people into activities which did not result in conversion and the growth of the church. To use McGavran's terminology, vast resources were being poured into the work of *perfecting those already converted*, to the neglect of the primary business of missions which is *conversion, making disciples.* In effect, whereas the people's movement style of mission meant that people became Christians while remaining in their own culture, the mission station style meant that people were being co-opted into the culture represented by the missionary, taught to accept as models of excellence the education, medicine, and technology of the

West. The church, centered in the foreign mission station, became a colony of a foreign culture. If this false approach is abandoned, if cultures are accepted as they are, and if the gospel is addressed to each cultural group in a form appropriate to it, then we can expect very rapid church growth. The life of a church, therefore, should be so ordered that becoming a Christian does not threaten the integrity of a culture or the cohesion of the cultural group. Thus, for example, the struggle of the church in South India to insist that caste differences be abandoned among Christians, and that Christian congregations should ideally unite people of different castes in one fellowship, is mistaken. In fact, it gravely inhibits church growth. It should be abandoned. Following what the Church Growth missiologists call the "homogenous unit principle" (HUP), people of one caste should be encouraged to form Christian congregations on a caste basis, for it is very difficult to contemplate conversion to Christianity if it means breaking the loyalties of the kinship group.

Although I find it necessary eventually to reject the Church Growth missiology as a total package, I want to say that I believe it contains important elements of truth. When McGavran and I were both serving as missionaries in India, his books came to me as illuminating my situation. I find marks of approval in the margins of my copies of his earliest works. He rightly saw that missionaries measure discipleship by standards derived not from the Scriptures but from their own European and American cultures and that there was a disastrous confusion between conversion and cultural change. One could cite, for example, the absurd rule enforced in some areas of Africa that a condition for full communicant membership was literacy. Jesus Christ came into the world to save literates. One could draw attention to the confusion of education with evangelism, to the fact that in thousands of villages of the Third World the school and the church were really only different names for the same activity, so that being a Christian meant being on the ladder of education of which the topmost rungs were of course entirely made of Western material. I have seen enough in my own missionary experience of church growth through spontaneous initiatives apart from any apparatus of schools to know that there was important truth in McGavran's thesis.

Yet it cannot be accepted in full. McGavran finds a biblical justification for his sharp distinction between "discipling" and "perfecting" in the text of Matthew 28:19-20, which instructs the apostles to "disciple the nations, baptizing and teaching." But, as David Bosch has pointed out, the text confutes any attempt to separate discipling and teaching (or perfecting as McGavran calls it): it defines discipling as baptizing and teaching. To suggest that discipling is one thing and teaching something else is to do violence to the text. Making a disciple by definition involves teaching. There can be no conversion which has any reality if it does not involve a change in perception and in behavior. In other words, conversion cannot leave culture unchanged.

But what kind of a change will it be? That is the crucial question. Here again we have to say that to give the true answer to that question requires a true doctrine of the work of the Holy Spirit. If the new kind of behavior which conversion must entail is something laid down unilaterally by the missionary upon the convert, then we are led into all the distortions which have cast missionaries in the role of destroyers of culture. What is the nature of the change which conversion necessarily entails? It is a change in perception, it is the U-turn which makes what seemed absurd or scandalous reveal itself as the wisdom and power of God. It is always something mysterious, something for which the human words and deeds of an evangelist may be the occasion but never the sufficient cause, something which can only be understood as the work of the sovereign Spirit of God. And so also the change in behavior. It is not submission to a new law imposed from without, but response to a new presence within, to the presence of the Spirit of God. When Levi on his conversion gave a feast to his friends, it was not obedience to a new command, but the overflow of a new Spirit. When Zacchaeus found that he was accepted by Jesus and immediately offered to give away his accumulated wealth, it was not because Jesus so ordered him; it was because joy constrained him. The new kind of life which follows conversion is not subservience to a new law but the fruit of the Spirit. New converts may surprise the missionary by the decisions they make — sometimes vehemently rejecting things which the missionary would not have questioned, sometimes retaining elements of culture which the missionary regards with suspicion. In every situation there will be conflicts of judgment about what are the priorities for change. Only those who are part of a living culture can fully feel the implication for good or evil of elements in that culture. The missionary has a role to play as the representative of the long Christian tradition. Ideally decisions are reached in fellowship. What is clear is that culture must neither be absolutized nor rejected. The interaction of gospel and culture will go on as long as the culture lives.

III

As I have been discussing the interpretation of the Matthean form of the Great Commission, it is appropriate to look briefly at another point of dispute about the same text. The command is to disciple the nations: *ta ethnē*. Much has been made of this, especially by German missiologists. The objective of missions, it is said, is not the conversion of individuals but of whole communities. As some of the most famous missionaries of recent times have found, like Christian Keysser in Papua-New Guinea and Bruno Gutmann in East Africa, there are some communities so tightly bound together that it is almost impossible — even were it desirable — to seek for the conversion of individuals. If conversion is to occur, it must be the whole community which turns together, so that not only individual lives but also the whole accepted custom of the tribe is changed. It is by accepting this model of missions that missions in the past hundred years have been instrumental in bringing into being strong indigenous churches in Papua-New Guinea, in Sumatra, and among the Chagga people of Tanzania and the Dalit in South India — which are truly people's movements. Somewhat similar ideas, though probably reached independently, have often appeared among those concerned with mission to sectors of public life in modern Western society. Those involved in modern industrial missions have tended to view with distaste the thought that they were looking for the conversion of individuals: they have addressed themselves rather to the structures of industry as such. Similar thinking can be found in the recent report on chaplaincy in Polytechnics entitled "Going Public." This entirely eschews the thought that chaplaincy in a Poly is in the business of individual conversion. It is concerned rather with the life of the Poly as a single corporate society. What is to be said about this?

Let me make two points. First: in spite of the well-known missionary hymn, this text does not instruct us to "baptize the nations." It tells us to disciple the nations (*ta ethnē* — neuter noun) and to do it by baptizing and teaching people (*autous* — personal not neuter). And there is

87

no other way by which human communities — whether a mountain tribe in Papua or the staff of the Polytechnic in England — can be discipled, unless people, individuals, are converted, turned around so as to become believers in the strange truth that the power and wisdom of God, the gracious rule of God, is present in its fullness in Jesus. In my own missionary experience I have been familiar with group movements which bring a whole village community to ask for baptism. And I am sure that in such communities it is better that the whole village should accept baptism together rather than that the wholeness of the community should be broken by baptizing some and rejecting others. But I know also that such group movements are sterile unless there is a sufficient number of people in the group who have been truly converted so that Christ is for them a reality supreme above all else. And I would suggest that the same principle applies to enterprises like industrial mission and Polytechnic chaplaincy. It is indeed true that a kind of conversion which involves only the private religious practice of the person converted and does not challenge or change the whole of their involvement in the life of the industry or the Polytechnic is irrelevant and can even be counterproductive insofar as it identifies Christian faith with a sort of abnegation of public duty. But if the work of chaplaincy in industry and in Polytechnics is only that of advocates for structural reform, they are purveyors of law rather than the gospel. What makes possible the transformation of a whole human community is the presence in it of people whose lives have been regenerated by the work of the Holy Spirit in the heart of the believer through the communication of the gospel.

And second: what exactly are "the nations"? Not, certainly, the seventy nations listed in the tenth chapter of Genesis. All of those have disappeared except the tribe of the children of Eber. And not the nation states which are currently the members constituting the United Nations Organization. Particular nations are not eternal and no particular ethnic grouping can claim an abiding missiological significance. I have heard Indian theologians using this text to call for a specifically Indian form of Christianity but in the same speech vehemently attacking the presence of caste loyalties in the church. But caste — the extended kinship group, the Indian counterpart of the tribe in Africa — has more claim to represent the nations of the Bible than the nation states which are largely the creation of European political and military power. A tribe in Papua may be — or may at one time have been — an isolated group commanding the total allegiance of its people. But in a modern society we owe loyalty to a number of groups — nation, trade union, university, professional guild, and many others. One of these cannot be exalted above all the others as the one which is to determine the style of our discipleship. The individual belongs not to one human group, one tribe, one nation, but to many.

These reflections lead, I think, to the following conclusions. We must not build too much on the fact that the object of the imperative verb "disciple" in the text is "the nations." There is no way in which human groupings, nations or tribes or industries or Polytechnics, can be discipled except as the people who compose them are converted, baptized, and enabled to live in the power of the Spirit. The emphasis of the text, seen in the light of the role of the public world in the thought of Israel, is not upon the specificity of nations as distinct human groupings, but upon the fact that the call of God now goes beyond Israel to the whole family of the descendants of Noah with whom the original covenant of blessing was made.

IV

In what I have said so far, I have taken most of my examples from what we call the Third World. And indeed most of the animated discussions among missiologists on the theme of gospel and culture tend to take their illustrations from Africa, Asia, or the South Seas. But the crucial illustration, the place where our theories on the subject must above all be tested, is in relation to our own culture, a culture of which we are a part. What does "discipling" mean to the cultures of which we are products, which shape the way *we* understand the world? Our problem here is not that the gospel appears as something foreign to our culture; it is that it has become so totally domesticated within our culture that its power to exercise a radically critical function is in question. Every attempt to communicate the gospel across a cultural divide has to find the narrow way between two errors: the first is to fail to communicate because one has not learned the language, has not entered deeply enough into the thought world of the other culture to make the message meaningful. The other is to identify oneself so completely with that thought world that one loses the possibility of challenging it. The message is heard merely as a summons to moral reformation or religious revival — not to the radical change of perception and direction which is conversion. It is often said that the failure of the Western churches is of the first kind: irrelevance, failure to make contact. I want to suggest, on the contrary, that it is a failure of the second kind, that the Christian churches of the West have been so co-opted into our culture that we have lost the power to challenge it.

Please permit an illustration from my experience as a young missionary in India. As I tried to understand Indian thought, studying it as an outsider, I soon came to realize that the doctrines of *karma* and *samsara,* doctrines which interpret human life on the analogy of the cyclical patterns that prevail in the natural world, were so fundamental to Indian thought for perhaps three thousand years that they were hardly ever called into question. They describe how things are and have always been. And so it was natural that Jesus would be comfortably fitted into this way of understanding the human situation. He is one of the long line of *avatars* who have come at the appropriate times to restore *Dharma.* In the hall of the Ramakrishna Mission where I used to go each week for study and discussion, the portrait of Jesus hung along with those of the other men of God, and worship was offered before his picture at the Christian festivals. To me as a foreign missionary it was clear that this was in no sense the conversion of India. It was the co-option of Jesus into the Indian thought world in such a way that *that* world went unchallenged and unchanged. *Karma* and *samsara* still rule. History is cyclical. One event in history cannot change the nature of reality. It may illuminate it, but it cannot change it. The perception of how things are remains undisturbed.

There is a similar process of co-option which effectively silences the gospel in our culture. One of the decisive marks of our culture, comparable in importance to the idea of *karma* and *samsara* in Indian thought, is the assumption that facts are one thing and values something else; that there is a public world of facts which everyone knows and a private world of beliefs and values where we do not expect everyone to agree; a world where pluralism reigns and a world where it does not; a world of affirmations about things which have been, as we say, scientifically established and which are therefore stated in the textbooks as facts which are true whether the readers believe or not, and a world of affirmations which have to be prefaced by the words "I believe," affirmations which we do not expect everyone to believe. That every human life is governed by the program encoded in the DNA molecule is a fact. That (to use the old phrase) the chief end of man is to glorify God and enjoy Him forever is in our culture not a fact but a belief held by some people. The former will be part of the school curriculum; the latter will not. Of course it is a fact that human beings have religious beliefs but the things they believe are not facts. Consequently, my affirmation about the chief end of man will find a place in the curriculum only — if at all — as one item in a course on the comparative study of religions. It has been silenced not by contradiction but by co-option, as effectively as it is neutralized by the inclusion of a picture of Jesus in the gallery of world religious teachers. The gospel cannot challenge the presuppositions which authorize its inclusion in a list of entities called "religions," any more than Jesus can step out of the picture in the hall of the Ramakrishna Mission and question the basis of its teaching. It can be studied as one of the many varieties of religious experience; it cannot challenge the presuppositions of that study.

There is a real danger that the Church Growth missiology can obscure the issue I am here trying to confront. If one follows McGavran in separating discipling from teaching; if one regards it as the primary purpose of mission to increase the number of Christians and treats such increase as the criterion of success, without posing all the time the more radical questions which the gospel puts to the common assumptions of our culture, if the dominical call to "repent" is translated as "turn away from your sins" and there is no understanding of that radical overturning of the world's ideas of sin and righteousness and judgment, then there can be rapid church growth; but the very success of the burgeoning congregations may actually incapacitate them for a radical encounter with the culture into which they fit so comfortably. If religion is an affair for the private life, it can flourish in a society governed by other assumptions, taking the characteristic form which we know so well — a series of voluntary societies made up of people who share the same religious tastes. In that form Christianity can flourish, but it cannot challenge the beliefs that control public life. It has been co-opted into the culture.

V

These reflections on the theme of gospel and culture suggest some final reflections on the first word of my title, the word conversion. It is not a popular word in the circles in which most of us who are part of the academic world move. It carries overtones of shallow emotionalism, manipulative evangelism, and narrow bigotry. There are real grounds for the suspicion of talk about conversion. And yet if we are faithful to Scripture we cannot avoid it. As I reminded you at the beginning, the initial summons of Jesus according to our oldest Gospel is a summons to be converted, to turn around, to face the other way. And yet we are uncomfortable with this. Is it not precisely the emphasis upon conversion which accounts for the bad reputation of missionaries as destroyers of culture? Has not the call to conversion been interpreted as a call to reject everything in the traditional culture because it was part of the world? Did turning to God not mean putting the world — and the traditional culture — behind you?

And this is not only a question affecting our view of the work of foreign missions. I find in this country, in discussion with clergy, a great desire to play down, to minimize the distinction between the church and the world, to emphasize the goodness of the world as God's creation and therefore to affirm the continuity between the good things of human culture and the perfection of them by grace in the life of the church. One of the axioms most often quoted in the discussions I have had is the one which affirms that grace does not reject nature but perfects it. In the Catholic wing of the churches, this is often quoted in attack upon what is perceived as a Protestant error — the drawing of a sharp line between the unconverted world and the converted church. What shall we say about this?

I have already touched on this in discussing the debate about continuity and discontinuity which followed the publication of Kraemer's great book fifty years ago. I used the analogy of the paradigm shifts in the natural sciences, as described by Thomas Kuhn in his book on the structure of scientific revolutions, to make the point that there is indeed a continuity, but it is a continuity visible only from the other side of the shift. The old paradigm cannot make sense of the new, but the new can make sense of the old. I think it is a true analogy: the man in Christ can rejoice in all the riches of human culture. But for many cultured people, the message of the cross is perceived only as an attack upon culture.

Everything depends upon the paradigm shift, upon the new way of seeing things. Without this, the message of the church becomes mere exhortation. And I fear that this in fact is what has happened. If one looks at church pronouncements about public issues, what is obvious is they consist in large part of moral exhortation. They are not in the indicative mood but in the imperative — or shall we say optative; they are not about what is the case, but about how we would behave if we were only more committed to good causes. And this corresponds to the dichotomy which I have identified as the most striking feature of our culture, the dichotomy between the world of facts and the world of values. The church is perceived as belonging to the second area, a good cause requiring the support of good people. It is not perceived as a body which radically challenges the accepted view of what is the case with another view of reality, with a claim to see what the majority of humankind do not see because they are facing the wrong way.

I remind you again of the mistranslation of Jesus' initial announcement of the gospel in Today's English Version. His summons to repent, to turn around, is a summons to be converted, to see things in a wholly new way, to a radical paradigm shift. To translate it by "turn away from your sins," thereby turning it into a mere moral exhortation, is to destroy the meaning of the summons, for — as the story unfolds — it becomes clear that it is precisely the sinners who understand and the righteous who do not. Truly it can be said of the first great British theologian that he, being dead, yet speaketh: I refer, of course, to Pelagius.

It is right to reject the kind of distinction between the church and the world which implies that the grace of God operates in the church and not outside, that the world of human culture outside the church is a wasteland from which God is absent. That is a monstrous falsehood. The Psalmist says that God's tender mercy is over all His works — and of course He is not talking about religion. Yet we know that there is a vast and terrible mass of evidence in the story of human society which seems to contradict this affirmation. It is from the other side of Good Friday and Easter that one can confidently make it. The true humanism is possible, and is only secure, from the standpoint of that strange victory in which death and destruction have been met and mastered.

Grace does indeed perfect nature, but only as nature is converted and baptized under the sign of the cross. Human culture is profoundly ambiguous, and always carries the seeds of its destruction. It stands with all human life under the law that the way to life is through death. To silence the call to conversion is no service to culture, for the true flowering of culture is on the farther side of conversion.

III. Church, World, Kingdom

I

In a memorable phrase during one of the debates about the proposed integration of the International Missionary Council with the World Council of Churches, that well-beloved German missionary Walter Freytag spoke of the "lost directness" of mission. For many people in an earlier period it seemed that the missionary calling was capable of a very simple definition: it was to go out to heathen lands afar, preach the gospel, and bring more and more to conversion, baptism, and membership in the church, the ark of salvation. Whether one approved of the enterprise or not, it was something clear and straightforward. It might be thought of (and often was) as something marginal to the main business of the church — a vocation for a few rare souls like Henry Martyn, heroic or crazy according to one's point of view; but it was clear and easily defined.

Today we have all learned that mission is not marginal to the life of the church but definitive of it, central to its being. Ecclesiastics today, unlike their predecessors fifty years ago, talk much about mission. In the most influential contemporary document on ecclesiology, the *Lumen Gentium* of Vatican II, the church is defined from the outset in missionary terms. The church is God's sending, His mission. It is in its very nature apostolic, missionary. But by the same shift of perspective, mission now often appears to be everything rather than something. It is the whole life of the church. In a justly popular series of posters the United Society for the Propagation of the Gospel has offered such a wide variety of images of mission that the word covers almost everything that a Christian might be interested in. Specifically, and this is where disquiet sets in, mission is defined so as to include not only humanitarian services of all kinds but also radical political action directed against established institutions and ruling powers. Partly because of the powerful witness of the Latin American liberation theologians, churches in many situations see revolutionary struggle against oppressive powers as the heart of their missionary calling; and the oppressed may be Third World peasants, urban blacks, or middle-class women. Missionaries, men and women, have been and are in the leadership of such revolutionary struggles in the Philippines, Guatemala, El Salvador, South Africa, and among the outcaste villages of India. For such missionaries it is unacceptable to define mission simply in terms of preaching the gospel, baptizing, and nourishing church growth. But for many other Christians it is at least odd to define mission in terms of radical politics.

The lost directness is manifest in another way. It is not just that the missionary normally goes to a place where the church already exists. He is not sent, so to speak, to confront the unconverted world directly. He goes, usually, to work as part of an already existing church. But it is not just this which accounts for the "lost directness." It is also that the boundary between church and world has become blurred. There is no longer a well-maintained boundary fence. We are more conscious of the fact that God is already at work in the world outside long before the missionary arrives. So, it is said, the first business of the missionary is not to preach but to listen, to open not his mouth but his eyes and his ears. I was recently in a gathering of clergy, recalling my experiences of preaching the gospel in Indian villages where the name of Jesus was hitherto unknown. I was gently rebuked and told that I had the wrong idea of a missionary. I should have kept my mouth shut and opened my ears to listen to them telling me what God was already doing in their lives. God was already there. My journey was unnecessary. And how often have we read stern warnings issued, for instance, to industrial chaplains to remember that they do not take Christ into the factory, for He is already there. Two phrases often heard in discussion about mission express the point. One speaks of "God at work in the world." The inference is that we do not initiate the movement; it is God's mission. God is already working in the world far beyond our little ecclesiastical ghettos. Our business is to go outside the church walls, become aware of what God is doing, and cooperate with Him. The other phrase is one which was popular in the 1960s: "the world sets the agenda." The gospel is not a pre-packaged commodity which we can simply deliver to the world: rather it comes alive, becomes really good news, at the point where people are, where it meets real questions, where it is — to use the blessed word — relevant. If our preaching is answering questions which the world is not asking, then, so the argument runs, it is futile.

A third set of terms may be added to this list of issues on which traditional pictures of mission have been challenged by some modern practice. The mission of Jesus, it is rightly said, was about the coming of the Kingdom, not about the establishment and expansion of the church. So, if we are to be faithful to Him, we should be more concerned with the Kingdom than with the church. What matters is not how many people are converted and baptized, and how slowly or rapidly church membership grows: what matters is that God's mercy and justice should be set forward in the life of the world. For many contemporary Christians, the Great Commission of Matthew 28 has been displaced by the Nazareth sermon of Luke 4. The mission of Jesus, and therefore our mission, is not to make disciples but rather to bring to the poor good news of liberation from poverty, to proclaim release to the captives, and liberty to the oppressed. If that is happening, the mission is being accomplished. That, and not the numerical growth of Christian churches, is the goal of missions.

Much of what I have been describing may seem to be, and is felt by many evangelical Christians to be, a deviation from the true nature of mission, a falling away from the primary work of evangelism to activities which may be worthy but are secondary. Our theme in this lecture is "mission then and now." Must we agree that what is called mission now is, like so many other things, not what it was then?

Let us consider these three issues in the following order: first, the role of missions in political action; second, the relation of church and Kingdom in missionary thinking and practice; third, the role of listening as opposed to proclaiming.

A recent book by a Dutch theologian bears the title *Everything Is Politics, but Politics Is Not Everything.* That could be aptly applied to the work of mission. In no time or place have missionaries worked in a political vacuum, has the work of missions been politically neutral. To accept a given political order is as much a political decision as to challenge it. Sometimes missionaries have judged the political order of the place where they worked simply by the criterion of its helpfulness or hostility to the work of evangelism. Often, to their credit, they have felt obliged to challenge the given order. In general they have favored whatever could create a stable society free from violence and civil war. Sometimes this meant that they refrained from anything which would upset the existing regime. Sometimes it meant that they welcomed the coming of a European power to put an end to chaos, or to such evils as the slave trade in Africa, widow burning in India, cannibalism in New Guinea, and the horrors of blackbirding in the South Seas. Some colonial governments regarded the presence of missionaries as an embarrassment because they interfered with the purely commercial interests of the Europeans; hence the exclusion of missionaries from the areas controlled by the East India Company, and hence the humiliations suffered by the early Lutheran missionaries from the Danish authorities in Tranquebar.

What is more significant is that missionaries were almost from the beginning drawn into works of education and healing. These led to vast enterprises in the development of improved forms of agriculture and of new industries to provide a source of livelihood for the new Christians who were often driven out of their traditional vocations. It was missionaries who introduced the cultivation of the cocoa plant in Ghana, and of tea and coffee in East Africa. The large three-volume work of James S. Dennis, published at the turn of the century with the title *Christian Missions and Social Progress*, shows what an enormous interest there was nearly a century ago in what we would now call development work. All this activity had political repercussions. In some cases — as among the untouchables of South India — it led to violent clashes between newly emancipated serfs and their masters.

The story of missions, from the days of Henry Martyn until now, is also punctuated with fierce internal debates about the propriety or otherwise of this massive involvement in social, economic, and political affairs. It is, of course, also hotly attacked from outside the church by those who see it as an illegitimate use of superior Western techniques and political influence to persuade the weaker elements in a society of the merits of Christianity. In a recent discussion between Christian missionaries and their Muslim counterparts, the latter expressed very strong resentment about the use — as they saw it — of mission hospitals in the Muslim lands as centers of Christian propaganda. I am not now referring to this issue, but to the internal debate among Christians about the large role of educational, medical, and socio-economic programs in the work of missions over the past two centuries. Over and over again the complaint is made that these have crowded out the one essential — namely, explicit evangelism. The powerful Church Growth school has this as one of its main contentions. Over and over again in missionary history, new bodies have been founded with the avowed intention of concentrating on pure evangelism, and over and over again they have in turn been drawn into other activities of the kind I have referred to.

And indeed it is the very nature of the gospel itself which always defeats these attempts to separate the word from the deed, to give one primacy over the other, because the gospel is precisely good news of the Word made flesh. If one looks at the original mission charge to the twelve apostles, as it is given in Matthew's Gospel (Matt. 10), the point becomes clear. The charge is, initially, to heal and to exorcise. Nothing is said about preaching. There follow the names of the twelve, and then the injunction: "As you go, preach, saying: 'The kingdom of heaven is at hand.'" Very clearly, the preaching is the explanation of the healing. There were others in the land with gifts of healing and exorcism. Is Jesus, then, just another of these charismatic healers? No: there is a deeper meaning. These happenings are signs of a new reality coming into the life of the world, a reality which calls for a radical response. The happenings are not self-explanatory. They can be misunderstood. They can even be ascribed to the devil. They need a word to explain them. On the other hand, if nothing is happening, then there is nothing to explain, and the preaching becomes mere words, empty of substance. The word has power where it makes plain the hidden meaning of the deed. The deed has power where the word brings understanding of the new reality of which it is a sign. To set word and deed against one another, and insist that one or the other has primacy, is futile. The announcing of the good news about the Kingdom is empty verbiage if there is nothing happening to make the news credible. On the other hand, the most admirable program for human welfare does not provide any substitute for the name of Jesus in whom God's reign has come. At its very best, such a program can be no more than a sign pointing toward the full reality which we encounter only when we encounter Him.

Missionaries do not have to apologize, then, for having become so deeply immersed in works of teaching, healing, and welfare, even though they have to repent of the fact that these have sometimes become a substitute for explicit witness to Jesus. But does the New Testament authorize us to define mission so that it includes not only such benevolent activities as schools and hospitals, farms and workshops, but also involvement in political action for the overthrow of oppressive structures of power? Does the Nazareth Manifesto, with its promise to set at liberty those who are oppressed, authorize us to include revolutionary political action within our definition of mission?

To ask that question is to enter a veritable minefield, and I am not confident about finding a safe route through it. Of course, as I have already said, we are inexcusably naïve if we do not recognize that all these activities which I have been describing have vast and often revolutionary consequences. Let me begin with something that suggests an affirmative answer to my question. When the risen Jesus said to the apostles "As the Father sent Me, so I send you" and showed them His hands and His side, He was identifying the mission upon which He sent them with the way of the cross (cf. John 20:19-23). And that way was — in one aspect — the way of total protest against the established powers. To announce the imminence of the Kingdom, to announce that God's reign of justice is about to break into the world, is necessarily to be on a collision course with the presently reigning powers. But this breaking in of God's reign does not take the form of a successful political movement to remove the reigning powers and replace them with rulers who will faithfully execute God's justice. It takes the form of a shameful and humiliating defeat, which, however, in the event of the resurrection is interpreted to chosen witnesses as the decisive victory of God's Kingdom. He reigns from the tree. So, as the apostle says, the principalities and powers have been unmasked, and their pretensions to wisdom shown to be false; they have been disarmed, but they have not been destroyed. They still exist and still have a function, but one which is authorized and therefore limited by the justice of God manifested in Jesus. To accept this sending, this mission defined by the scars of the passion, must mean that the missionary church will continue that protest against, that unmasking of, the hypocrisy, cruelty, and greed which infects the exercise of all political power, and yet will accept the fact that the visible end of that road is a cross, and that it is only beyond the cross, beyond all earthly programs, beyond death, that the victory of the justice of God will be made manifest.

Unless the radical otherworldliness of the gospel message is acknowledged, the real role of the church in politics will be hopelessly compromised. Instead of a movement of radical protest, suffering, and hope, there will merely be a naïve and ineffectual utopianism. The reign of God which is the subject of the gospel message is *not* the end product of political development; and every attempt to confuse the two results in disappointment and disillusionment. One can make the point very simply (perhaps crudely) by considering the Beatitudes. Why are those called happy who are poor, oppressed, persecuted, hungry, meek? Simply because it is they who, in the new age, will be rich, free, and joyful. Most of them will still be poor and hungry, oppressed and tearful for all their earthly lives. They are happy because something infinitely good is promised to them in the new world. This is unpopular doctrine — "pie in the sky when you die." One might think that even that is better than pie for those of your great-grandchildren who survive the revolution and belong to the right party. However, the point is that this otherworldliness is what the teaching of Jesus clearly seems to imply.

What, then, is its relation to the mission of the church in the world? Not quietism. Not passive submission to the rule of injustice and greed and hypocrisy. The earthly ministry of Jesus is the sufficient refutation of such a conclusion. Or it ought to be — for it must be confessed that the church has often preached quietism, in the times when churchmen were in the seats of power. Jesus, according to Saint John, was manifested to destroy the works of the devil, not to submit to them. His whole ministry is portrayed in the Gospels as a mighty onslaught on the works of the devil — whether these took the form of sickness and demon possession among the people, or of hypocrisy, cruelty, and hardheartedness among the rulers. And His whole ministry is interpreted as the breaking in of the reign of God into the life of the world, to release those whom Satan has bound. To quote the title of a famous book, His was "the faith that rebels." No sick person brought to Jesus was ever told to accept his sickness as God's will. Always Jesus was moved to act — moved, it seems, both by pity and by anger, because Satan had so grievously oppressed God's children. Right to the very end, His hand is stretched out to heal. Even on the cross, He speaks the word that brings release to a dying murderer. And yet, as the mocking spectator said, He who saved others could not, or did not, save Himself. At the end — but only at the end — there is a cry of submission: "Father, into Thy hands I commend my spirit." The coming of the Kingdom lies in His Father's hands, on the other side of death and defeat. The earthly ministry of Jesus is not the launching of a movement which will gradually transform the world into the Kingdom of God. It is, rather, a showing forth, within the confines of the present age, of the reality which constitutes the age to come — the reality of God's reign.

And so when the risen Jesus says to His disciples "As the Father sent Me, so I send you" and shows them His hands and His side, He is commissioning them to continue what He came to do: to embody and to announce, within the limits of the present age, subject as it is to sin and death, the reality of the new age, of God's reign of justice and mercy. With that commissioning goes also the empowering of the Holy Spirit — so that, by the same Spirit whose anointing enabled Jesus to do works of healing and deliverance, the church could likewise be empowered. But the outcome will not be a successful program for the progressive transformation of this present world into the new world. "He showed them His hands and His side." The breaking into history of the kingly power of God will indeed create happenings which challenge the powers that oppress and dehumanize, which unmask the pretensions of principalities and powers; yet the ultimate sign of the Kingdom in the life of this world is the cross — the cross of Him who in the resurrection is manifested as Lord over all powers, even the power of death.

Plainly, therefore, the company which is entrusted with the commission to embody and to announce the presence of the Kingdom cannot take the form of a political movement. Politics is a sphere in which one is concerned both with ideas about human welfare, about justice and freedom, and also with the use of coercion to bring these ideas to embodiment in the life of society. Politics is always a mixture of both. Political change is not brought about by purely rational and moral persuasion. And even the most brutal use of violence, whether to defend or to attack an established order, is always obliged to cover its nakedness by some appeal to justice and freedom. The church is necessarily involved in politics, in that it is entrusted with a message concerning human well-being, concerning the true content of justice and freedom. But the church betrays its calling when it seeks to become an organ of coercion. Its role in politics is different and unique. It is to embody and to announce the presence of the Kingdom under the sign of the cross and in the power of the resurrection. And this brings me to the second of the three issues I have identified, namely, the relation of church and Kingdom in the missionary calling.

II

I find myself in agreement with much of the criticism which is directed against a missionary practice that puts all the emphasis on the church and its growth. Behind such practice lies, I think, a wrong conception of election as election for the sake of the elect. This is the error which the prophets of Israel had over and over again to attack. God called and chose Israel not just for Israel's sake, but that Israel might be His witness to the nations. And when God calls a man or woman to become a disciple of Jesus, a believer, a member of the church, it is in order that the church may be a sign and instrument and foretaste of His kingly and fatherly rule for all peoples. Church growth is therefore not an end in itself. There have been, and there are, situations where churches grow rapidly through evangelistic preaching, conversion, and baptism, but where the church functions not as a witness for God's justice but as a reinforcement and legitimization of injustice and oppression. In such situations it is right to protest, to point out that the central theme of the gospel is the imminent presence of God's Kingdom of justice and freedom; and that a church which itself condones and profits by injustice, even if it grows rapidly, is a sign against the Kingdom and not for it.

But if church growth cannot be posited as the primary goal of missions, it is equally necessary to insist that the fulfillment of Christ's commission must include the call to a total allegiance to Jesus, and to commitment to the company of His people, the company that bears His name, the church. Without this, talk about the Kingdom is too easily co-opted into a utopianism which owes more to the nineteenth-century doctrine of progress than to the essentially apocalyptic teaching of the New Testament about the Kingdom. This utopianism can come in various forms according to local circumstances. In the relatively free and comfortable countries of the "first world" it is often marked by innocence to the point of naïveté about the realities of power. In the harsher conditions of the Third World, the Marxist version of utopia has much more persuasive power. But in both situations the distinctiveness of the church's witness to the Kingdom is compromised.

Church growth is not the primary goal of missions, but without the church there cannot be authentic mission. It is only in the church that the true otherworldliness of the gospel is held together with its true this-worldliness. For the church is that body which has Jesus as its only head, and it is in Jesus that the Kingdom is present. The name of Jesus cannot be used as an adjunct to some progressive or revolutionary ideology. Every concept of the Kingdom has to be continuously tested in the light of the revelation of the Kingdom given uniquely and once and for all in the ministry, death, and resurrection of Jesus. It is only through union with Him that we live as citizens of the new age while at the same time taking our full share of responsibility for life in the present age for our fellow human beings and for our earth. In the life of the church, in the power of the Spirit continually renewed through word and sacrament and mutual pastoral care, we are enabled to share in Christ's bearing of the *karma* of humanity, and so to share by way of foretaste in the liberation He has won. Through Him we are enabled to share in the compassion of the Almighty Father who does not use power to enforce obedience but waits with infinite patience and mercy for our repentance.

This otherworldly reference of the church is essential to its this-worldly mission. If that is absent, the church is merely a minor disturbance in the ongoing business of the world. Of course, this otherworldliness is a cause of offense. Of course, those passionately engaged in the struggles for justice and freedom will condemn the church insofar as it fails to identify itself wholly with one side or other in the battle of the moment. And of course, it is also very hard for the church to resist the temptation to secure itself by keeping out of the battle; or to pretend that it is doing so by aligning itself with those who have the power.

It is very hard to say what has to be said here without falling into error on one side or the other. I want to affirm primarily that the church is a witness to a reality which transcends the present world and its struggles for power, and yet that this witness is always relevant to these struggles. So one has to reject two false positions. One is the position, sometimes championed by radical exponents of political theology, that there is no truth apart from or beyond the mental constructs which are formed by our involvement in society; that questions of truth can be settled by asking the question: In whose interest is this thought developed? Certainly, that is in all circumstances a proper question. Certainly, all human attempts to grasp the truth are shaped by the social location in which the attempt is made. But all serious thinking is an effort to reach out beyond one's location to the truth which is truth for all. If there is no such truth, then rational and moral debate ends, and there is no way to settle matters except by force, by the elimination of the other party. The church bears witness to a revelation of truth by which all claims to truth are to be tested, but through which — in the cross of Christ which is its central point — there is forgiveness for all the lies by which we have torn our world to pieces. This revelation forbids us to make an absolute identification of any human cause with the reign of God. In the presence of the cross there are no innocent parties and no innocent classes. And there is no body which can make this witness except the church, defined as it is simply by its acknowledgment of the supreme lordship of the crucified and risen Jesus. We are all together found guilty and all together forgiven. The church is called to be the place where that is actually happening. That means also that it is a place where all of us recognize that the victory of any cause, however just, is not the victory of God; where we have a sober awareness that our success always contains the seeds of failure, that the powerless and exploited of one generation can become the oppressors of the next. But it also means that this sober recognition in no way diminishes the confident hope with which we act, because we can know that the consummation of all the struggles of human history will be the work of God beyond the grave into which we and all our works must descend, to be raised, purged, and renewed for a Kingdom more glorious than we can conceive.

But the opposite temptation lurks on the other side of the faith, the temptation to interpret the otherworldly character of the Kingdom as a cause for quietism, for a cowardly evasion of the struggle, for failing to challenge or expose the works of darkness, for a selfish religion which looks to the salvation of one's own soul and is not moved to share the agony of God's compassion for a tormented world. That has been the typical error of churches when they were comfortably ensconced in the established order. If we resist the temptation and insist that discipleship means following Jesus in challenging the works of the evil one wherever they appear, then we shall sometimes find Christians taking opposite sides on political issues. A church which has lost the essential otherworldly reference at the center of its whole life will be unable to endure the resulting tensions. Yet in spite of what is said from the side of liberation theology, I would affirm that to be able to hold these tensions is part of the essential witness of the church to the Kingdom. We live under the cross. I am not overlooking the fact that there may be occasions where a particular position is to be judged not merely as error but as apostasy and calls for excommunication. One cannot exclude that possibility. Yet a review of history suggests that the church has been in general too quick to use the ultimate weapon than too slow. God has not ratified all of the church's anathemas.

I conclude that while church growth is not the primary goal of missions, it remains central to the missionary calling of the church that the gospel calls for a radical conversion of heart and mind, and a full commitment to the life of a community which is identified by its bearing the name of Jesus. The church is not to be identified with the Kingdom, but is properly the sign and foretaste of the kingdom. When we set Kingdom issues against church issues, we are always in danger of defining the Kingdom in terms of some contemporary ideology and not in terms of the manifestation of the Kingdom in the incarnate, crucified, and risen Jesus. The apocalyptic strand in the teaching of the New Testament cannot be removed without destroying the strength of the whole. There is no straight line from the politics of this world, from the programs and projects in which we invest our energies, to the Kingdom of God. The holy city is a gift from God, coming from above. Its coming lies on the other side of death — the death of the human person and the death and dissolution of all our political structures and of the cosmic frame itself. God's final reckoning with our apostasy cannot mean less than this, as the last book in our Bibles reminds us with such searing clarity. The church exists as sign and foretaste of the gift that is promised; in all its members it is called to act now in the light of the promised future: that is its proper this-worldliness. But the church maintains at its heart, through the word and sacraments of the gospel, its witness to a reality which is not of this world. Only the church can give that witness. Without it, our this-worldly programs are only a minor disturbance in the world's business, offering illusory hopes that are not changing the realities of the human situation before God. The church has a real purchase on the world's life only insofar as it finds a point of reference beyond the life of this world. Only the hope which enters into the inner shrine behind the curtain provides us with an anchor which cannot be moved by any storm or tide.

III

As the apostle tells us, we have to give an account of our hope. We have to name it. We have to speak, to tell the name that identifies our hope. Does this suggest arrogance? Does a proper humility require us rather to be silent and to listen to what God is saying now in the events and movements of our time?

There are many who press this view upon us. In my own experience, the most vivid case of this was in the passionate debate in the Uppsala Assembly of the WCC in 1968 — between those who wanted to direct attention to the millions who had never heard the gospel and those who saw mission as involvement in the struggle for human liberation wherever it is going on. The final report showed that it was the second group that had won the day. A long section entitled "Opportunities for Mission" deals not with unevangelized peoples but with situations of revolutionary struggle. Finally, the church itself is identified as a prime target for mission because its structures are oppressive. In the human struggle for liberation, God is already at work: the mission of the church is to work with God in this struggle.

What is to be said to this? Surely, in the first place, to affirm that God is already at work in the world, His judgments are in all the earth. He casts down Pharaoh and He raises up Cyrus. His tender mercies are over all His works. He clothes the lilies and He feeds the birds. He sends the rain on just and unjust alike. All things and all people have their being by His grace and in the freedom that He gives. As the prologue to the Fourth Gospel affirms with unforgettable clarity, Jesus — the living Word of God who is God — is the light that illumines every human being without exception and the source and secret of their life. So He is no stranger to any human being, for all things were made through Him.

Why, then, is there any need to introduce Him, to proclaim Him, to announce His name? Is He not there already before the missionary comes? Yes, He was in the world. Yes, but the world knew Him not. That is the dark mystery of our fallen world. He is present, but unknown, unrecognized. He is there, but He has to come, and when He comes, He is not received or acknowledged. The light shines in the darkness, and the darkness can neither comprehend nor overthrow it, though it tries to do so.

The gospel tells the story of what happened when the true light came into the world, the only light, the light that shines on every human being, the light in which things are seen as they are and reality is distinguished from illusion. Those who were confident that they could see turn out to be the blind, and those who knew that they were blind receive their sight. The light shows up the illusions of human wisdom and godliness and political shrewdness. It overturns human confidence that we can know how and where God is at work in the world. It invites us to believe that the victory of God is achieved in the rejection and shame and suffering of the cross.

What does this say to us about the balance between our speaking and our listening? I think we have to admit that we have often been guilty of a kind of speaking which was — so to say — from a distance, which contradicted the manner of the incarnation in that it was not spoken from within the situation of those to whom it was addressed. It was the Word made flesh who preached the good news of the coming of the Kingdom. And, as I said earlier, when He commissioned His disciples to go out and to preach the Kingdom, He first authorized them to exercise a ministry of deliverance, and He made it clear that the preaching was the interpretation of what was happening through that ministry. Moreover, He warned them that they, the bearers of the powers of the Kingdom, must expect rejection, suffering, and death. So the word of the preacher is spoken out of a deep and costly involvement in the human struggle against the forces that dehumanize and destroy.

And yet, the Word remains sovereign. In His lowly subjection to the powers, Christ is lord over them. The word of the gospel retains its sovereign freedom. The world sets the agenda in the sense that Christ's ministry is exercised in response to felt human needs — hunger, sickness, blindness. Yet the action of Jesus always sets the human situation in a new perspective. The deepest need of the Galilean crowd is not, as they think, the bread that fills the stomach for a day, but the bread that gives eternal life. The deepest need of the paralyzed boy is not that he be liberated to take up his bed and walk, but that he be set free from sin. In the end it is He, Jesus, who unveils the real agenda. It is only in the true light that the human situation is truly understood.

We think we know what our needs are. The missionary has studied the situation and thinks that he knows what the urgent issues are, where the new movements are beginning, where the opportunities for change are springing up. These attempts to understand the world's needs and hopes are not to be despised. But their role is secondary. The word of the gospel has its own sovereign freedom and is capable of surprising the missionary. The one who encounters Jesus in the gospel and in the church for the first time will often hear in his conscience a word that the missionary could know nothing about. The gospel is not in our control. The living Word is free and sovereign, and therefore it is right and proper in every situation to bear witness to Him who is the light of the world, the light in which we can see things as they really are.

Certainly, God is at work in the world, both to build and to pull down, both to plant and to uproot. But when, as so often happens, we suppose that whatever looks like the wave of the future is to be identified as the work of the Holy Spirit, we are already a long way down the road to a pagan worship of power. God is at work in the world, but the world in its wisdom does not know God. It has been so from the beginning, and it will always be so, that the word of the cross is foolishness to the wise of this world and a scandal to the pious of this world, but for those whom God calls to be witnesses against the world for the sake of the world, it is the power and wisdom of God. To speak that word to all who will hear is not arrogance: it is but responsible stewardship, and — more than that — it is the grateful offering of love to the One who so loved the world.

GOSPEL AND CULTURE

Address delivered by Lesslie Newbigin
to The World Conference on Mission and Evangelism
Salvador de Bahia, Brazil
December 1996

The Gospel . . .

I'm very grateful indeed for the generosity of the World Council of Churches in inviting me as a guest. I'm sorry that I was not able to be here for the beginning, but I have done my homework and read all the preparatory documents. I want just to say one thing which has struck me in reading through the documents and listening to some of the discussion.

We have talked a great deal about culture, and rightly so. I think we have used the word "gospel" without giving as much attention as we need to the question of what exactly we mean by that word. We don't mean Christianity. Christianity is what generations of us have made of the gospel, and we know we have often made a mess of it. We're not talking about religious experience either, because that also is a very ambivalent affair. We're talking about a factual statement. Namely, that at a certain point in history, the history of this world, God who is the author, the sustainer, the goal of all that exists, of all being and all meaning and all truth, has become present in our human history as the man Jesus, whom we can know and whom we can love and serve; and that by His incarnation, His ministry, His death and resurrection, He has finally broken the powers that oppress us and has created a space and a time in which we who are unholy can nevertheless live in fellowship with God who is holy.

Now these are factual statements about something which has happened. It is of course perfectly possible to say, "I don't believe it," or it is possible to say, "Well, that's one of the stories that people tell to explain the human situation." That is quite possible; and if one takes that position, then the matter is clear. We know where we stand. We can disagree but we can respect one another and do many things in common. But if it is true, if it is actually true that God has done those things which we repeat in our worship and in our hymns and in our liturgies, then it is certainly the most important fact in the world and one which we cannot keep to ourselves, one which has to be communicated. And it has to be communicated for a very special reason: the implication of it, as the risen Jesus Himself said (Matt. 28:18), is that the final authority lies with Him: "All authority in heaven and on earth is given to Me."

All of us need to know who is finally in charge. As far as the great majority of the people among whom I live are concerned, it is taken for granted that the final authority is the free market. The free market is the power against which even the largest governments confess themselves to be powerless. It is the sovereign power ruling public life. And while of course we all talk about moral values, and while we talk about the need for justice and compassion and human dignity and so forth, yet we are constantly reminded that in what is called the real world, these things do not have final say — that the final power lies with the free market. And the free market is a useful servant, but when it claims total mastery over human life, we know what the consequences are. If it is true that all authority is given to Jesus, and that He has thereby created a space and a time in which, in spite of the powers that seem to control us, we can obey Him, then to refrain from telling other people that this is so is not merely to betray the trust that has been given to us by our Lord, but it is also collusion with the occupying power. It is colluding with that power which deceives human beings into believing that the final authority lies for example with the free market. And that is why it seems to be fundamental that we place at the center of our concern for mission the simple responsibility to tell that story.

Now, God forgive me, we know about the sins of the old missionaries. I ought to know a lot about it because I am an old missionary and I have committed most of those sins, and I am deeply sorry for it. But it would be a strange response to that acknowledgment if I said that I will refrain from talking about Jesus and will offer my own life as a witness that will enable people to believe that something else is in power. That would indeed be a very strange conclusion to draw. I want of course, perhaps on another occasion, to talk a little more about the way in which the gospel relates to our culture, because that brings up a tremendous number of difficult issues which I find fascinating and important. But I want now just to continue on this one point. The specific responsibility which has been given to the church and to nobody else is the responsibility to bear witness to the reality of Jesus' victory. Of course there is an enormous amount that we also must do. The whole vast range of responsibilities which is so well summed up in our new "trinitarian" formula — justice, peace, and the integrity of creation — these are things in which we can share and must share with people of all faiths and ideologies, whoever they may be. They are part of our common responsibility as human beings and insofar as we neglect them, we certainly contradict the gospel that we preach. But that which has been committed to the church exclusively, and which no other agency will perform, is the responsibility to tell this story.

Now I know how easy it is to oversimplify. I know that the responsibilities of politics and economics have to be taken with utter seriousness. Whatever else we do for people — to come to know Jesus, to love Him, to serve Him, to honor Him, to obey Him — *that* is the greatest thing that we can do for anyone and it is the specific thing entrusted to us. It must be the center of our missions.

. . . and Culture

If we accept the fact that the gospel is a factual story about what God has done, we have immediately to say that that story has to be told in a human language. And language is the very heart of culture. It is the key to culture. And therefore there is no gospel which is not already embodied in a culture. But the question always is: What is the relation between the two? If one takes perhaps the simplest statement of the gospel in the English language, "Jesus is Lord," how do we understand that sentence? Does it mean that we understand Jesus as a lord in the way that a lord is understood in England — that is to say, someone who exercises power and has a seat in the House of Lords? Or do we recognize that our whole conception of lordship will have to be revised in the light of Jesus? And that of course will only happen if we expose ourselves to Jesus in such a way that our ordinary everyday use of the word lord is completely changed. That is why Jesus said to His disciples that they were to call no man lord; no one was to be called lord except Jesus. In other words, the question is whether the word Jesus redefines the word lord or whether the word lord defines Jesus.

On Saturday, as we stood on the dockside there, we had a vivid sense of what happens when the second thing takes place. The message of Jesus as Lord which was brought by the Portuguese, and expressed in the kind of rule that they established, arose out of that domestication of the gospel within European culture which led Europeans to see Jesus as lord in the sense that we understand lordship apart from Him. And that is why in this case the Christian message comes as bad news — though perhaps in fairness to the Portuguese we should remember that that domestication of the gospel in their society was the result of hundreds of years of struggle to reverse the Muslim military conquests of the old Christendom and the invasion of Southern Europe.

If I may give another example which concerns the cross-cultural communication of the gospel: I have done a good deal of street preaching in my life and I have often stood in a street to preach the gospel where the name of Jesus is quite unknown. It is no use mentioning the name of Jesus because no one knows what that means, but I have to use the word God. Of course I must find one of the many Tamil words for God and there are many words. And when I use one of those words, I know that in my hearers' minds they will be thinking of perhaps Shiva or Vishnu or Murugan or Subramanya or Ganesha or Hanuman. They will certainly not be thinking of the one whom I think of when I say the word God, the one I have learned to know through Jesus Christ. So what difference has my preaching made? So far, none at all. It will only make a difference when I begin to tell stories about what this God has done. Then you begin to see that God is different from what we thought, because you come to know who a person really is only by understanding that person's life, knowing how she behaves, how she responds in different situations, by interacting with her. And so it is only as the story is told and retold and retold that the new content, if you like, to the word God begins to appear. And of course it is a slow process which goes on and is never completed, but there is always that struggle between the two possibilities that our existing culture determines our understanding of God or that what is revealed to us in the gospel determines our culture. That is, as I say, a very long process which is never complete and is always continuing.

The most powerful and pervasive of all the cultures of the world at the present time is that one which has been developed in Europe in the past two or three hundred years and which has created a global unity based on the science, the technology, and the ideology of the free market. This culture is so overwhelmingly dominant that the question of the relation of the gospel to this culture is one of supreme importance. In the past two hundred years European missionaries have given much attention to studying the cultures of non-European peoples with a view to communicating the gospel to them. They have unfortunately not given so much time to understanding this culture within which the gospel has been so long domesticated. And that is a very, very difficult undertaking, a very painful undertaking.

I am going to raise one particular issue which I have never raised in public before and which I did not intend to raise when I came to Salvador. It is connected with this ribbon on my wrist. When we stood in the old slave market on Saturday morning on those rough stones which had felt the weight of the bare and bruised and shackled feet of countless of our fellow human beings, when we stood in that place so heavy with human sin and human suffering and we were asked to spend two minutes in silence waiting for what the Spirit might say to us, I thought first how unbelievable that Christians could have connived in that inhuman trade; and then there came to my mind the question: Will it not be the case that perhaps our great-grandchildren will be equally astonished at the way in which we in our generation, in our so-called modern, Western, rich, developed culture, connive at the wholesale slaughter of unborn children in the name of that central idol of our culture — freedom of choice? I know — and as I say, I have never raised that issue in public before, but I do so because I was told to do so — I know that to raise it is exceedingly painful, as painful as was the struggle against the slave trade, as painful as was the World Council's program to combat racism. But I have discharged that commission. In the context of this Conference it is simply one example of the costliness of that attempt to ensure that the gospel is not domesticated within our cultures, but continually challenges our culture.

That is why — whether we are talking about our own culture or about another one — the crucial question is whether we tell the story, whether we continue to recount the mighty acts of God, whether we continue over and over and over again to read and reread and ponder the story of Jesus, because it is only the telling of the story that can change the meaning of the words we use and the concepts that we entertain. I have said that this so-called Western, modern, scientific, free market culture is the most powerful in the world at the present time. There is one serious challenger at the present time — Islam. Islam, with a courage that should put us Christians to shame, is openly challenging the claim that the free market and all its ideology is what rules the world, claiming as we do that God is in control.

And, as I say, we should be thankful for that challenge. We should ask ourselves why we have not been equally courageous. Perhaps part of the explanation is that we know we have been so much domesticated within this Western culture that we do not have the courage to dissociate ourselves from it. But we know also that there is a profound differ-ence between the way in which Islam and the gospel respectively chal-lenge this reigning culture. For Islam the will of God is to be done here and now in the political order, where Islam secures control of the politi-cal order. Then dissent, disobedience, disbelief, is punished in the se-verest way, and there are some of us here who know from bitter experi-ence how terribly harsh can be the experience of Christians living in such situations; and I am personally ashamed of the silence of our pub-lic media in my own country about the sufferings of Christians in some Islamic societies.

The Christian gospel, on the other hand, affirms that the manifes-tation of the sovereignty of God was made not in an overwhelming dis-play of power but in the humiliation of the cross. Moreover, that aton-ing deed on the cross, which was in fact not defeat but victory, has been made known not as a great public demonstration, which would mean the end of human history, but as a secret communicated to a very small company chosen to be witnesses, so that there could be a space and a time within which there is freedom, freedom to dissent, freedom to dis-believe, even freedom to blaspheme, so that there could be freedom for a freely given allegiance, so that the rule of God, the kingdom of God, would not be a matter of coerced obedience, but of freely given love and obedience, the obedience of loving children.

And it seems to me that in the century that lies ahead of us these are the three major factors which will compete for the allegiance of the human family: the gospel, the free market, and Islam. I take it that the globalization of the whole human family is probably irreversible in the near future, that we must expect increasingly to see ourselves as one global city. I will not say a village because it is not a village. As to Islam: while the other great world faiths are deeply significant and worthy of respect, none of them makes that same claim for universal allegiance. As to the free market: the crucial question is going to be whether the Christian church can recover its confidence in the gospel in order to be able to challenge with confidence the enormous power of this ideology which now rules us. We are dealing here with an idol, the idol of the free market, and idols do not respond to moral persuasion. They are cast out only by the living God, and it is only the power of the gospel in the last analysis which can dethrone idols and which can create the pos-sibility of a free society — a free society which is pluralist in the sense that there is freedom to dissent. The secular model has claimed to provide freedom but it cannot sustain that claim. It has been successful only insofar as it has been sustained by the remaining power of the Christian tradition; and as that tradition weakens, the secular society is unable to defend itself either against the rising religious fundamentalisms or against dissent into moral anarchy and hopelessness.

The Christian gospel affirms that, not in spite of but because of our faith, we are required to provide space for disobedience, for dissent, for disbelief, in the faith that God in His own way and in His own time will manifest His rule. Only that faith in the long run can sustain a truly free society. And that, I think, indicates the very center of our calling as Christians — to recover confidence in the gospel as the power of God for salvation. And please, please: by salvation we do not mean that privatized commodity which the market economy offers us, a personal future for each one of us. By salvation the Bible means the final and glorious consummation of God's whole purpose for His whole creation. And if that is our calling, I would make two final points.

The first is: I plead, I plead that we stop arguing about whether or not other people are going to be saved. I do not believe that that is our business. I do not believe that we have a mandate to settle those questions. We know from the teaching of Jesus that one thing is sure — that at the end there will be surprises; that those who thought they were in will be out, and those who thought they were out will be in. The Bible as a whole and the teaching of Jesus give to us both immensely universalistic visions of the all-embracing power of God to save and to heal, but also and especially in the teaching of Jesus very, very harsh warnings about the possibility of losing the way, about the possibility of being lost, about the broad and inclusive way that leads to destruction and the narrow way, the hard way, that leads to life. And we have the testimony of Saint Paul, who can write on the one hand that nothing can separate me from the love of Christ, and on the other hand: I buffet my body and keep it under, lest having preached to others, I myself should be lost. I do not think it is our business to discuss the question whether other people are being saved. In that case there will be the final question: What then is the point of missions?

That, I think, brings us to the very heart of the matter. What is the point of missions? And the answer I believe quite simply is the glory of God. If God has done those things which we repeat in our creed, if God has so loved the world that He gave His only begotten Son, what is our response to that? Is it an argument about who is going to be saved? Surely not. It is thanksgiving. It is the question, how can I glorify God? How can I respond to that matchless gift? And mission is acting out that question. It is seeking so to witness to the love of God that there may be a response, that this love of God may not go forever unrequited, that it may not be forever spurned, that there may be throughout the world those who turn their faces to God and give Him thanks and glorify Him. The glory of God is the purpose, the goal of mission, and our one aim is that we should praise and glorify Him.

I find it strange that conferences about mission and evangelism are often pervaded (I won't say this of this one but of many that I've known) by a kind of anxiety and guilt — as though this were a program that we have a responsibility to carry out and about which we've not been very successful. Isn't it remarkable that according to the New Testament the whole thing begins with an enormous explosion of joy? The disciples returned to Jerusalem with great joy and were continually in the temple praising God! It seems to me, the resurrection of Jesus was a kind of nuclear explosion which sent out a radioactive cloud, not lethal but life-giving, and that the mission of the church is simply the continuing communication of that joy — joy in the Lord.